11/9/97

To our own resident Anglophile —
good bedside reading —
Gzy.

ROYAL GARDENS

ROYAL GARDENS

ROY STRONG

PHOTOGRAPHS BY ANDREW LAWSON

POCKET BOOKS

New York   London   Toronto   Sydney   Tokyo   Singapore

POCKET BOOKS, a division of Simon & Schuster Inc.
1230 Avenue of the Americas, New York, NY 10020

Library of Congress Cataloging-in-Publication Data

Strong, Roy C.
 Royal gardens / by Roy Strong.
  p.   cm.
 ISBN 0–671–79594–5 : $40.00
 1. Gardens — Great Britain — History.   2. Gardens — Great Britain–
–Pictorial works.   3. Great Britain — Kings and rulers.   I. Title.
SB466.G7S76   1992
712′.6′0941 — dc20   92–22698
                                                             CIP

First Pocket Books Hardcover Printing November 1993

10 9 8 7 6 5 4 3 2 1

POCKET and colophon are registered trademarks of
Simon & Schuster Inc.

Printed in Great Britain

Originally published in Great Britain jointly by
Conran Octopus Limited and BBC Books in 1992

ENDPAPERS Buckingham Palace gardens in 1831.
HALF TITLE PAGE The dolphin fountain near the Orangery at Hampton
Court which was made in the 1680s for Mary II.
FRONTISPIECE The rose garden at Highgrove House which was planted
in the 1980s by Prince Charles.
TITLE PAGE A lead cistern made for Charles II, now used as a planter at
Windsor Castle.
CONTENTS PAGE An ornamental alcove in Kensington Gardens made for
William III.

CONTENTS

INTRODUCTION

Gardens are a powerful and unique expression of human personality. And nowhere is this more forcefully evident than in the history of royal gardens. For four centuries British monarchs and their consorts have not only sought consolation and privacy in the glades and bowers of their gardens but have also used them to express some of their profoundest hopes and aspirations. For a few, gardening was even an all-consuming passion. George III's queen, Charlotte, may have been paid tribute to as the country's leading female botanist but the truth behind this was that 'botanizing' gave her and her unmarried daughters some sort of life away from the tragedy of a king who was insane. For Edward VII's beautiful queen, Alexandra, the gardens of Sandringham with their cornucopia of fragrant flowers gave solace to a woman whose life was blighted by deafness. For her parents-in-law, Victoria and Albert, their gardens at Osborne and Balmoral were a pure expression of what was a love match, so much so that after the Prince Consort's early death they were kept unchanged for forty years as a memorial to him.

Often figures who seem almost dull on the pages of history take on a new aspect when placed in the context of their gardens. Queen Anne, that least romantic of Stuart monarchs, when stricken by the death of her only surviving child, was carried out into her garden daily to assuage her grief. Her sister, Mary II, dominated by her austere husband, William III, only seems to come to life in her love of exotic plants and her need to be constantly supplied with bouquets of fresh flowers. Their strange marriage found its fulfilment not in children, for there were none, but in the joint creation of perhaps the most spectacular series of royal gardens ever made, at Het Loo in Holland and in England at Hampton Court and Kensington.

Gardens open a door not only into a private world but also into the theatre of politics and power. Charles II's gardens were laid out with all speed after the Restoration in 1660 to act as arenas in which he could meet his new subjects and re-establish the monarchy. Caroline of Ansbach, George II's queen, adorned hers with buildings whose political message enraged the opposition to the Crown. Her daughter-in-law, Augusta of Saxe-Gotha, wife of a Prince of Wales who died young, laid out Kew Gardens in celebration of the military victories which laid the foundations of the British Empire. George IV used his gardens as a backdrop to create a world which had been destroyed by the French Revolution and in which he could act out a fantasy. Even in our own age royal gardens have had their political context, for the gardening passion of George VI and the Queen Mother provided ideal material to help paper over the cracks made in the image of the monarchy by Edward VIII's abdication.

This is above all a book about royal gardeners. Some royal figures will inevitably therefore be missing, for as in any family not everyone is a gardener. George II and George V, for example, had not a flicker of interest. Indeed the shortest way possible around the Chelsea Flower Show often had to be found for George V. Nor will the reader find here gardens which just happen to be within the royal orbit, such as the Savill Gardens in Windsor Great Park or the Dutch Garden at Kensington Palace. The focus is on the personal, social and political aspects of the royal gardens, although their aesthetic aspect also finds a place in the story. Most of the great gardening names are here, from André Mollet to 'Capability' Brown, but not all of them: Gertrude Jekyll, for example, was never taken up.

And why does the story begin in 1660? The answer lies in the Civil War which broke out in 1642, in the aftermath of which not only was the King brought to trial and executed but also the monarchy was abolished and its palaces despoiled. The great heritage of Tudor and early Stuart gardens, Nonsuch, Richmond, Greenwich, Hampton Court and Whitehall, either completely vanished or fell into neglect. The heir to the throne, the future Charles II, would only have had distant memories of these gardens. He was twelve when the war started and most of the following years were spent in impoverished exile abroad in the Netherlands and, above all, in France at the court of Louis XIV, where a new garden style was about to enter its apogee and dominate Europe. He would, however, have been made aware of gardens in England through his mother, Henrietta Maria, for she had laid out two in the latest fashion at Somerset House and Wimbledon. It was she too who had twice brought the great French gardener, André Mollet, to England. It is hardly surprising, therefore, that when the Prince returned as King it was to Mollet that he turned, taking up the story of royal gardening where it had been left off in 1642.

BUCKINGHAM PALACE, GLIMPSED ACROSS THE LAKE, A VIEW WHICH HAS remained virtually unchanged since the gardens and palace were remodelled for George IV over a century and a half ago.

THE THEATRE OF THE COURT

CHARLES II

Charles II (1630–85) was thirty when he was restored to the throne in 1660. Tall, over six feet, and swarthy, he was a gregarious man who used his abundant charm to full effect, whether to political or amatory ends. His unceasing zest for life made him an appealing ruler, leading and enjoying the social round of the upper classes, one made up of field sports and lavish entertaining. He disliked reading and paperwork as much as he did any major confrontation. Exile and poverty had bred in him the flexibility of the willow and he would bend with the wind to ensure the continuance of the good life. And in that he indulged to the full, extravagant in his expenditure on both jewels and mistresses. He was a king made for the baroque age. Although he was the most accessible of rulers, at the same time he demanded the exact observance of every detail of court etiquette and ceremonial. Moreover, his tastes were already fully developed, for his formative years had been passed at the court of the young Louis XIV which set the style for the whole of Europe.

When Charles returned to England from exile in the spring of 1660 there

CHARLES II BEING PRESENTED WITH A PINEAPPLE BY A KNEELING FIGURE traditionally identified as John Rose, one of the Royal Gardeners. This detail from a painting by Hendrik Danckaerts, after 1670, is the first known portrayal of a gardener with a monarch.

CONCEIVED ON A VAST SCALE, THE LONG WALK WHICH STRETCHES SOUTH from Windsor Castle is a double avenue of trees no less than three miles long. It was originally planted with elms between 1683 and 1685, the year that the King died. It remains, although replanted with chestnuts, the best maintained legacy of Charles II's contribution to royal gardens.

were no royal gardens. During the Commonwealth virtually all of them had been sold off with the palaces, and destroyed. Only Tudor Hampton Court and Whitehall (which was to burn down in 1698) survived in some depleted form but to all intents and purposes the King had to start again. Charles's garden tastes had been formed in France by the gardens restored and altered by his grandfather, Henri IV. And Charles faced precisely the same task as Henri had: to create a new court life after over a decade of civil war. The royal palaces and their gardens were seen as having a major role to play in taming the aristocracy with a new form of elegant social life and the garden became a series of alfresco rooms to entertain and parade in.

The Mollet family played a key part in this development. Before the advent of André le Nôtre, they dominated French garden-making. Claude Mollet, who died c. 1649, had become gardener to Henri IV in 1595 and of his many sons, André and Gabriel both eventually settled in England, while Pierre and Claude II remained in royal service in France. Through André's travels and work in England, Holland and Sweden, the Mollets had already established French garden style throughout Europe. That style was associated above all with the development of the parterre, which was the supreme expression of seventeenth-century garden art. A parterre was a geometric ornamental garden on one level which had evolved during the Renaissance but reached its classic formula in France at this period. The main form it took was known as a *parterre de broderie* or embroidered parterre, a symmetrical geometric pattern in clipped green box, often of great complexity, set against coloured grounds made of brickdust, gravel, blue cobalt, sand, even coal dust and ground bones. These elaborate compositions, demonstrations of splendour, were sited beneath the main rooms of the house, which were on the first floor, enabling a full appreciation of the pattern.

But it was not the parterre which Charles II initially imported to England but something else which was characteristically French, the monumental canal. In 1607 Henri IV had begun the construction of the Grand Canal at the palace of Fontainebleau (1200 metres [1313 yards] long and 40 metres [44 yards] wide), edged with stone and stretching eastwards from the Grand Jardin of the Valois. It was lined on either side with avenues of elm. The function of this expanse of water was to act as a 'theatre' for the court and in October 1609 Henri IV and his son, the Dauphin, sailed along it before the assembled aristrocracy. A description in August 1661 records 'tout le beau Monde de la Cour' either aboard a magnificent boat floating along its waters or riding along the avenues either side on horseback or in carriages. And it was two canals of precisely this kind which Charles II started to make almost immediately on his return, responding to an urgent need to create such a 'theatre' for the newly reconstituted British court.

The first canal was in St James's Park, which stretched between the two Tudor palaces of Whitehall and St James's.

The park was for the hunt and even after it was redesigned it was to continue to be used for hunting. The task of building the canal and re-laying out St James's Park was entrusted to André Mollet, who had laid out the garden of Charles's mother, Henrietta Maria, at Wimbledon on the eve of the Civil War. He had gone on to gather further acclaim for his gardens for Prince Maurice in the Netherlands and for Queen Christina in Stockholm. In 1658 he had returned to England with his brother Gabriel and in June 1661 they would be awarded the post of King's Gardeners at St James's Palace. The digging of the long canal had, however, already started in September 1660, only four months after the Restoration, showing how urgently it was felt such a courtly public arena was needed.

André Mollet's highly influential book *Le Jardin de Plaisir* (1651), which had appeared in French, Swedish and German, described the new garden style which sought to draw house and garden into a total unity based on a central axis. Radiating avenues and walks ran to and from this axis and the whole was contained within a tree-lined rectangle. To reconcile the lay-out of St James's with such design principles, it has, however, to be viewed as relating not to St James's Palace but to Whitehall.

Charles had chosen Whitehall as his seat of government and was to spend his reign in a series of frustrated attempts to build a new palace fit for a monarch in the baroque age. Apart from the Banqueting House built for Charles I, Whitehall was much as Henry VIII had left it, a rambling redbrick assemblage of buildings of no great distinction. The architect John Webb's early designs for a new Whitehall Palace show that it was to be symmetrical with an east-west axis covering the entire site of the old Tudor palace and with the new state apartments looking down on to St James's Park. The new canal was thus sited with the potential of making it answerable to that façade which, if it had ever been built, would certainly have had a great parterre beneath its windows.

As it was, the canal and the other features planted by Mollet look strange and unresolved, for all that they related to was a flight of wooden stairs leading down from the old tiltyard gallery on to what we know today as Horseguards Parade. The canal, and the avenues of trees that flanked it, led away from Whitehall by way of a *patte d'oie*, or goose-foot. This was an ingenious way of both creating an enclosed public space – a semicircle of trees – and, through the avenues that radiated off it, providing articulation to the parkland beyond, from where the vistas would have led back to the new palace.

Further to the north, parallel to the façade of St James's, a second series of avenues was laid out. These were for the fashionable game of *paille maille*, which was a summer pastime and therefore called for shady trees on either side of the long arena. The King was adept at the game. He was also a great walker and later in life would take two walks each day in the park at exact times which were prompted by looking at his watch. These were the occasions when he was at his most

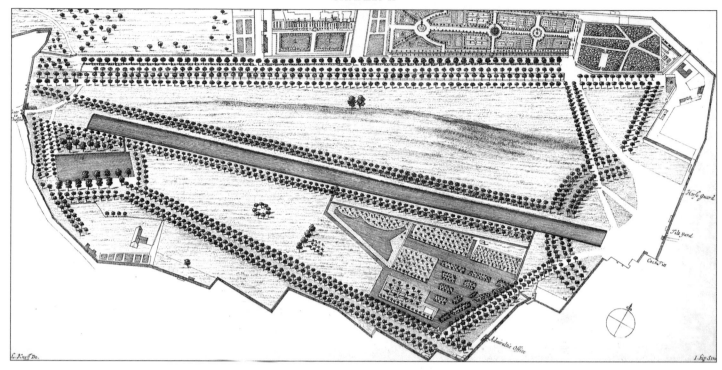

THE GROUNDPLAN OF ST JAMES'S Park by Leonard Knyff of 1707 (*above*) shows how it was laid out for Charles II in the 1660s. Although the main lines of the canal and avenues appear to converge on the site of Buckingham Palace on the left, in fact they radiated out from the semicircle of trees in front of Whitehall to the right. Whitehall was the old Tudor palace and seat of government; immediately following Charles's restoration in 1660 plans were made to demolish the old palace and replace it with a new one in the classical style whose garden front would be St James's Park. To the north, at the top, is a series of small formal gardens laid out for Charles II in front of the palace of St James's. This palace had been built by Henry VIII to overlook what was a royal deer park for the hunt.

THE BIRD'S EYE VIEW (*left*), A detail from a print of 1720 by John Kip, looks eastwards along the ancestor of the present Mall, the route to Buckingham Palace from Trafalgar Square. To the left are the gardens of St James's Palace: a pair of simple turf parterres with statues at their centres and, beyond, further to the east, the spectacular formal Privy Garden. The main long narrow rectangular area is laid out for the fashionable game of *paille maille* (from which Pall Mall takes its name), which involved hitting a ball with a mallet through a hoop. Double avenues on either side provided shade for the players and cool walks for the onlookers.

A VIEW TOWARDS WHITEHALL FROM ST JAMES'S PARK BY HENDRIK
Danckaerts of c.1668 (above) shows the eastern end of the newly dug
canal which was an essential part of Charles II's scheme to transform
the park into an elegant public arena. The painting captures the social
function fulfilled by the new garden: the King is seen on one of his
daily walks which gave opportunities for encounters with a wider
spectrum of established society than could be accommodated in the
palace. Of the cluster of buildings which made up Whitehall Palace,
only the magnificent Banqueting House, seen on the left, built in the
classical style for Charles I by Inigo Jones, still stands today.

approachable to everyone else who paraded there. The poet,
Edmund Waller, eulogized the royal reordering of 'this fair Park,
from what it was before'.

Other pleasures within this fashionable enclave included an
aviary, a menagerie and a series of duck ponds for shooting. The
canal also came into its own in winter when it became a skating
rink. The diarists paint a vivid picture of its success. Evelyn
records skaters on the canal in December 1662, admiring their
'strange, and wonderful dexterity'. He visited the menagerie in
February 1665, examining a pelican and a stork, and describing
'Deer of several countries, white, spotted like leopards, antelope,

an elk, red deer, roebucks, stags, guinny goats; arabian sheep
etc'; 'very diverting' he records 'among such a concourse of
soldiers, guards and people'. Pepys too gives us glimpses of this
new court life: the Duke of York playing *paille maille* in April
1661, and in September walking himself with his wife to see
'the brave alterations'.

Until well into the middle of the eighteenth century, St
James's Park remained an essential meeting place between ruler
and subject. But although the park was the ancestor of today's
public space, admission to it was only by way of locked gates.
Accessibility varied under different monarchs: it was liberal
under Charles II, although closed during both the plague and the
great political scares of the Popish and Bye Plots, while under
Queen Anne admittance was grudging. To close off all such
access to the monarch was politically dangerous for St James's
Park gave the late Stuart monarchy its largest 'room' in which to
meet the established classes. Access to the King was a jealously
guarded privilege, for the whole system of political patronage
depended on it, and more people had access to the park than
the more exclusive milieu of the palace. When George II's
Queen, Caroline, wished to convert the area into a private
garden for herself, she abandoned the idea after Sir Robert
Walpole told her the cost would be 'only three CROWNS'.

After André Mollet's death in *c.* 1665, a rare English translation of his book appeared, *The Garden of Pleasure* (1670). It included one engraving not in any of the earlier editions, a plan of the Privy Garden which lay to the east of St James's Palace. As it could not be viewed from above Mollet had to abandon any hope of planting a *parterre de broderie*. Instead, between 1660 and 1661, he devised a garden of two parts, rigidly symmetrical, each side mirror-imaging the other along the central axis. Near the palace were *bosquets*, geometrically planted copses, centred on an ancient oak left to commemorate an escape by Charles II at Boscobel after his defeat in a battle in the Civil War, when he had hidden in the branches of an oak tree to avoid the parliamentary soldiers. The remainder of the garden was divided into sections in which turf, at that time a highly valued garden feature, was cut into patterns, enclosed by hedges and set off by cypress trees, reflecting the English love of simple verdant turf as opposed to the French predilection for complex pattern and show. There were also lavish plantings of dwarf fruit trees, roses, vines and flowers. By the opening of the next century Charles II's formal gardens were to be obliterated by those made for Marlborough House and Carlton House, and in the first quarter of the nineteenth century the formality of the park would be swept away under the aegis of George IV to look much as it does today.

The highly successful formula of St James's was repeated a year later, in 1661, at the old Tudor palace of Hampton Court. The work was prompted by the negotiations for the King's marriage to Catherine of Braganza, daughter of the King of Portugal. On the signature of the marriage treaty in June 1661, a massive refurbishment of the palace began in order to receive the new bride. It could not be foreseen that this docile Catholic princess, poorly educated beyond an excessive piety, would prove barren and would become a peripheral figure in the life of the court. The Queen was to end up living most of her time away from her husband at Somerset House, leaving him, together with a succession of mistresses, to set the style.

As at Whitehall, a new arena had to be created at Hampton Court for the diversion of the court and the only side on which the garden could reasonably expand was eastwards. John Evelyn in June 1662 describes the new-found splendour of the palace interiors glittering with gold and silver and then goes on to the gardens. 'The Park formerly a flat, naked piece of ground,' he writes, 'now planted with sweet rows of lime-trees, and the canal for water near perfected'. In the King's Privy Garden he admired the fountain by Le Sueur which had been made for Charles II's mother at Somerset House. Cromwell had moved it here and, later, Queen Anne was to move it again. There was a hornbeam walk which he deemed 'very observable' on account of 'the perplexed twining of the trees' and a parterre called Paradise with a pretty banqueting house. The gardens as a whole, however, were 'too narrow for such a Palace'.

The Great Canal was the sensational novelty. It was dug in

THE STATUE OF THE BORGHESE WARRIOR (*above*) WAS ONE OF FOUR bronze casts made from Roman antiques by Hubert Le Sueur for Charles I's formal garden at St James's Palace. It was then placed by Charles II at the head of the new canal in St James's Park (*opposite*). Later still it was moved to Hampton Court gardens by William III, and now stands in the East Terrace Garden at Windsor.

the winter of 1661–62 at the huge cost of £1446 and was centred on the new gilded balcony of the Queen's bedroom. Seven hundred and fifty-eight lime trees lined its banks and formed a huge semicircle nearer the palace. Water had never been used in gardens on this gigantic scale in England before. It was a mile long. Although truncated in the reign of William and Mary in order to create the Fountain Garden, the Long Water, as it is now called, remains one of the most staggering and least recognized masterpieces of landscape design in the country. And from May to August 1662 it provided the decor for the court *en fête* in celebration of the royal marriage.

A month after these celebrations all energies were turned towards another Tudor palace, Greenwich. Like Whitehall, it was to be demolished and replaced by a new palace designed by John Webb. Only one block was ever built and the whole

THE LONG WATER AT HAMPTON COURT WAS DUG DURING THE WINTER OF 1661–62 in time to welcome Charles II's bride, Catherine of Braganza. The contemporary view (*above*), a detail from a painting by Hendrik Danckaerts of *c*.1665–7, looks towards the east façade of the old Tudor palace, which Wren was destined to replace. The canal, which came far closer to the palace than it does today, was centred on the Queen's bedroom window, from where it could be seen striking out into the previously untamed landscape to the east. On either side of it there was a double avenue of limes. The whole complex was designed for a similar purpose to the one at St James's, for the court to ride and stroll along, or to float on the waters in barges. Before this time there had been a series of small pleasure gardens to the south of the palace and kitchen gardens to the north but the creation of the canal signalled the huge expansion typical of palace gardens in the seventeenth century. This is an almost miraculous and under-appreciated survival of what is the grandest formal use of water in garden-making in Stuart England.

palace project was finally abandoned in 1674, when the first block was boarded up; but by then the work on the gardens was very far advanced. These all radiated outwards from the elegant palladian Queen's House, designed by Inigo Jones before the Civil War, which occupied a position at the centre of the proposed new palace. Improvements were already under way in the winter of 1661–62, when a flight of twelve huge grass steps, 36 metres (40 yards) wide, were built up the scarp of the hill behind the Queen's House. They were flanked by a planting of Scots pine brought south by the Duke of Albemarle. It was clear from this that the garden was to be of a new kind, using landscaping and planting to enhance the perspective and embrace the hillside behind.

This garden was intended to be very different from either St James's or Hampton Court, for the keenly francophile King had learnt of the miracles achieved by André Le Nôtre at the château of Vaux-le-Vicomte. Charles was probably made aware of him through his sister, Henriette d'Angleterre. A letter from England to Louis XIV's Foreign Minister in May 1662 records: 'The King of England, walking two days ago in St James's Park, and talking of the alterations he hoped to make in his gardens, especially at Greenwich, notified that he would require the help of Le Nôtre, who has charge of the King's gardens, and he begged me to write to His Majesty to ask that he would allow him to make the journey to England.' The French King replied that 'although I have need of Le Nôtre continually . . . I will certainly allow him to make the journey to England since the King so desires'.

Two years later, in October 1664, Charles wrote to his sister: 'Pray lett le Nostre go on with the modell [plan] and only tell him this addition, that I can bring water to the top of the hill, so that he may add much to the beauty of the descent by a cascade of water.' Although there is no evidence that Le Nôtre actually came to England, this indicates that his involvement went on for some three years and that plans must have gone to and fro across the Channel.

In 1662, when the initial request was made, Le Nôtre had just entered into royal service thanks to the fame of his achievement at Vaux-le-Vicomte. That was his first great garden, made between 1656 and 1661, and the team which created it went on to make Versailles. At Vaux, Le Nôtre had taken up the principles evolved by Mollet to establish what was recognized as the classic garden style of *le grand siècle*. Mollet's gardens were rectangles divided by allées into a grid system that was arranged symmetrically on a central axis. Within this rigid grid any garden progressed through a set succession of features. First came

the *parterre de broderie*, the intricate pattern made from ribbons of box hedging, which was sited beneath the windows of the house. Next would come areas of turf cut into complex geometric patterns called *parterres de gazon* or *gazon coupé*. Then came *bosquets*, formal woodland planted to create walks, 'rooms', labyrinths, even theatres of greenery. Le Nôtre took that format and orchestrated it to create subtle changes of level within the huge level platform on which the house stood.

It was a style full of the utmost sophistication of effect in the way of surprise and vista. Water, treated either as flat mirrors or as fountains, united the various parts and formed focal points. And, above all, the scale became huge, a deliberate demonstration of an owner's wealth and prestige. The manipulation of space, with all lines converging on the house, was a perfect expression in garden terms of Louis XIV's dictum: *L'état, c'est moi*.

Greenwich was a contracted version of Vaux; the main difference was the terrain. Whereas Le Nôtre's gardens were mostly created on the flat countryside of the Ile de France, at Greenwich he had to contend with a steep hillside. The feature which was to unite the ascending parkland and the grand parterre on the level site created at the back of the Queen's House was a series of cascades down the hill. How astonishing this would have been if ever made! As it is, the great allées of his scheme and the sculpturing of the terrain can still be seen today, an under-appreciated masterpiece of baroque garden design that has survived because the palace was never built. If it had been, Le Nôtre's park would have been swept away by the landscape style in the next century.

The central feature of the garden was to be the first large baroque parterre ever planted in England, for which there is a design by Le Nôtre that is very close to that at Vaux. Work proceeded, at the immense cost of £2000, to level the site for the parterre and form terraced walks around its three sides. In January 1664 five hundred 'great Elme Trees' were planted on the terrace walks where strolling courtiers would be able to admire the patterns of the parterre below. But alas the parterre never materialized. After 7600 trees were planted to form the park, the project stopped. With Charles II's abandonment of Greenwich the development of the parterre had to await the accession of his niece, Mary II, in 1689.

The King, however, had other palace projects. On 29 September 1670 John Evelyn noted: 'Windsor was going to be repaired, being exceedingly ragged and ruinous'; the King spent his time there hunting and also walking in the Great Park, 'which he was now planting with walks of trees, etc.'. If

Hampton Court and Whitehall endowed Charles II with the glamour of the Tudors, Windsor surrounded him with an even more potent aura, for not only was his father, the Royal Martyr, Charles I, buried there, still awaiting his shrine, but Windsor was the seat of chivalry, where the rites and ceremonies of the medieval Order of the Garter were assiduously cultivated by the restored monarchy.

In November 1673 Hugh May was appointed Comptroller of the Windsor Office of Works and under his direction the castle interior was transformed into a baroque paradise in which, through illusionistic painting, the King's wildest aspirations to absolute rule were realized. It was not, however, until 1680 that attention was turned to the grounds. A baroque palace had to be the culmination of the surrounding landscape, with avenues and allées radiating from it. In order to achieve that essential effect, land was needed to both the north and south of the palace and in December 1680 the decision was made to start acquiring the necessary land. During the King's lifetime the area between the castle and the Thames was not obtained but enough land to the north was purchased to make it possible to proceed with the grandiose avenue now known as the Long Walk. Between January 1683 and June 1685, £3645 16s 11½d was expended on the project. The enormous number of 1864 elm trees was planted in four rows along a length of three miles, creating an avenue that directly linked the castle to the park for the first time. To protect the avenue, ditches were dug either side and whitethorn hedges planted.

The work was carried out by Moses Cook and George London. Cook had been gardener at Cassiobury Park to the Earl of Essex, 'that great encourager of planting', as Evelyn called him. Cassiobury had been rebuilt in the 1670s by Hugh May, who had been appointed Supervisor of the Royal Gardeners in 1670, and the garden was laid out with Moses Cook in a style that moved on from the tight rectangles of André Mollet to strike out across the landscape with huge avenues and rides. Cook's partner at Windsor, George London, had begun his life as an apprentice to another Royal Gardener, John Rose, and had been sent to France to study the gardens of Le Nôtre. In 1681 Cook and London joined forces with Roger Looker, Catherine of Braganza's gardener, and John Field, gardener to the Earl of Bedford at Woburn Abbey, to establish the Brompton Park Nursery (on the site of the present Victoria & Albert Museum). Looker died in 1685, Field in 1687 and in 1689 Cook retired and sold his share to Henry Wise, thus instigating the famous partnership of London and Wise which would dominate British and royal garden-making into the next century.

The Long Walk at Windsor is one of George London's earliest works and the new commission must have stemmed from Hugh May's association with Cook in the 1670s. The principle of the avenue cutting through the landscape, experimented with at Cassiobury, was enlarged on a dramatic scale. Charles II's plans for Windsor both inside and out were, however, not

THE LONG WALK AT WINDSOR (*above*), PLANTED IN 1683–5, penetrates three miles into the park. Its purpose was to make the surrounding landscape seem subservient to the castle – and hence to the King himself.

CHARLES II'S MONOGRAM ON A LEAD WATER CISTERN (*opposite*), ONE OF A pair now used as seasonal plant containers in the East Terrace Garden at Windsor.

completed by the time he died in 1685, and indeed, the saga of the King's gardens reads like one of dashed hopes. No complete new royal garden was ever made for the King, only a series of half-finished and abandoned projects. Remarkably, however, most of them survive. Of all eras of royal garden-making, this one remains perhaps least recognized, for collectively these garden survivals are the British equivalent of Versailles. So much of the formal garden heritage was to be swept away in the next century that the existence virtually unchanged of Charles II's gardens remains something of a miracle, albeit one crying out for greater care, conservation and restoration. The Long Water at Hampton Court is as stunning as any lake by 'Capability' Brown and precedes them all by nearly a century. The French would accord Greenwich the reverence they give to Fontainebleau or Versailles; even in its unfinished and unrestored state it stands as a great masterpiece of formal garden design. And the Long Walk at Windsor is Britain's noblest avenue.

IN 1662 WORK ON A NEW PALACE at Greenwich began. For the design of the garden Charles II turned to the newly emergent master of the French classical garden style, André Le Nôtre, who was at that moment engaged on laying out Versailles for Louis XIV. Although work on Greenwich came to a halt in 1674, and only later in the century did the building take the form we know today as the Royal Naval College, a bird's eye view by John Kip of 1699 (*right*) and an aerial view today (*opposite*) show how much of Le Nôtre's great structural framework has survived. The Queen's House, built by Inigo Jones before the Civil War, is seen here in the centre behind the Naval College. Beyond this there was to have been a large rectangular parterre. The central axis lined by double avenues of trees, which leads to the top of the hill, was to have been the course for a great cascade of water. More avenues strike out into the park making a harmonious symmetrical composition.

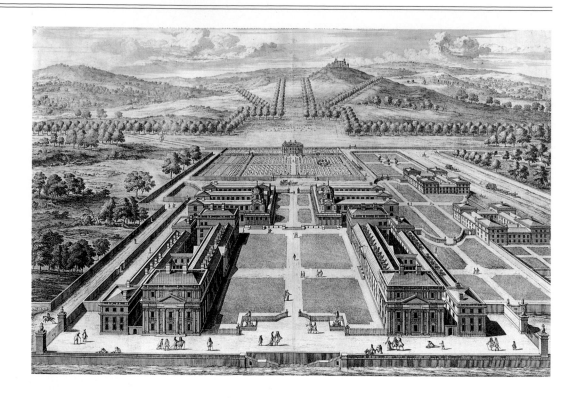

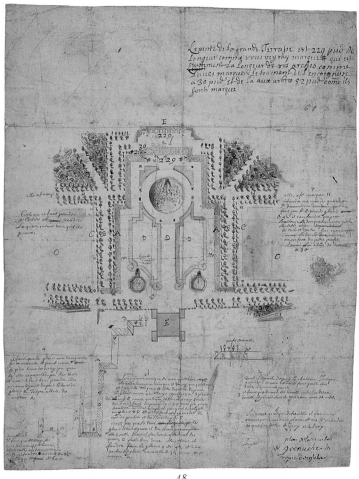

THIS DESIGN FOR THE GARDENS AT Greenwich Palace by André Le Nôtre of 1662 (*left*) is the only one to survive. As far as we know Le Nôtre never came to England in person, but must have sent a whole series of proposals and sketches. If the new palace had been built, its garden façade would have looked down on the parterre (D), the design for which included a very large circular fountain and two smaller ones, and was enclosed on three sides by tree-lined walks (B) on raised terraces. The series of arches (E) indicate a grotto which would have been at the end of the proposed cascade.

PRODIGALITY AND POWER

WILLIAM III, MARY II AND QUEEN ANNE

The 'Glorious Revolution' of 1688 ushered in an equally glorious era of royal gardening. It was prefaced, however, by the brief and disastrous reign of Charles II's brother, James, Duke of York, who in 1685 had succeeded as James II. His rash attempt to Catholicize the kingdom led to his downfall. The King was forced to flee, seeking refuge at the court of Louis XIV, while his Protestant nephew, William of Orange (1650–1702), Stadtholder of the Netherlands, landed in England at the head of an army. Invited to come by the great Protestant magnates, he was met with popular acclamation and although his wife Mary had the real claim to the throne, William

WILLIAM III AND MARY II IN c.1685 AND QUEEN ANNE IN 1683; DETAILS
of portraits by Willem Wissing. William and Mary and then Mary's
sister Anne reigned over a period in which the royal gardens reached a
splendour never since eclipsed.

MAGNIFICENT IRONWORK ENCLOSES AND ENHANCES THE PRIVY GARDEN
at Hampton Court. Designed by Jean Tijou for William and Mary, the
screens provided an intriguing transparent wall and were also ideal
vehicles for the display of regal heraldry and symbols within
the garden.

would accept nothing less than that they should rule as joint sovereigns. Mary (1662–94) was the elder of James II's daughters, and only surviving children, by his first wife; his newly born son by his second, Catholic wife, was discounted. Like her sister Anne (1665–1715), who would succeed as Queen on William's death, Mary had been brought up Protestant and her unshakeable devotion to the Protestant faith made her a welcome new monarch after her father's Catholicism. She and her husband were crowned in April 1689 and together, as William III and Mary II, they inaugurated not only a new reign but a new garden style.

William was the son of Charles I's daughter, Mary, who had been married to the Stadtholder of the Netherlands on the eve of the Civil War. His father had died shortly before his birth and his mother when he was only ten; as Prince of the House of Orange he inherited rich estates and by the time he married Mary in 1677, he had already proved himself a statesman and a brilliant soldier, leading his armies to victory over the French. As a personality, however, he was cold and reserved, his manners stiff and formal. He was also dogged by ill-health throughout his life; indeed his chronic asthma was to condition his choice of residences and his love of the fresh unpolluted air of gardens.

His wife, twelve years younger and only fifteen when she married him, was very different in temperament, high-spirited, romantic and something of a chatterbox. They made a strange couple even to look at, for Mary at almost six feet towered over her small, stern-looking husband. Yet the marriage turned out to be surprisingly successful. They remained childless but were held together by a mutual passion for building, interior decoration and above all gardening.

When the couple arrived in England they already had over a decade and a half of garden-making behind them and they brought with them the garden style associated with Holland's golden age. It sprang from the response earlier in the century to the Italian villa gardens of the Veneto by Palladio and Scamozzi, modified later by the response to the French classical style of Le Nôtre. Both sources of inspiration were tempered by the traditions and terrain of the Netherlands. First and foremost was the difference of scale: a Dutch garden, however magnificent,

retained a domesticity absent from its French counterpart. Water, which often presented horrendous engineering problems in France, was abundant in a country intersected by canals and this made it possible to compartment gardens not by built structures or hedges but by water. Also, the flatness of the land, with virtually no changes of level, meant that there was a strong interest in ground-level pattern, leading to the development of every conceivable form of parterre.

Mathematical principles clearly underlay the structure of any Dutch garden, reflecting the intellectual climate of the country with its pursuit of scientific inquiry. This was a period of Dutch mercantile dominance through the port of Amsterdam and the great Dutch trading companies, and new plants poured into the country from the Cape, India and the New World. They were collected and appreciated with a fervour associated today with works of art and rare plants changed hands at huge prices. Around the middle of the century, when tulipomania was at its height, a single bulb could change hands at a price many times that of a Dutch landscape painting.

All of the residences which William inherited from his father had spectacular gardens, which he proceeded to alter and enlarge. Two in particular, Honselaarsdijk and Het Loo, are important because they had such an influence on the work William and Mary were to undertake at Hampton Court and Kensington.

The garden at Honselaarsdijk had been laid out in the 1620s by William's father, Frederick Henry, on strongly geometrical lines. Canals defined the domain, dividing it up into a series of rectangles at the heart of which were two circular tunnel arbours of hornbeam. In the 1630s the French designer, André Mollet, added two elaborate parterres in the latest manner on either side of the house: one a highly complex *parterre de broderie*, swirling patterns in clipped box, the other a turf parterre which consisted of areas of grass cut into geometric patterns and also set against a background of coloured gravels.

William and Mary settled at Honselaarsdijk after their marriage and it was here that Mary first developed her garden passion. A special flower garden was laid out for her and the gardener was given instructions in November 1678 'if possible

THE GARDEN OF HET LOO,
William and Mary's palace in
Holland, was laid out in the
1680s and excavated and re-
created in the 1980s. Today it
provides a rare experience of
the authentic reality of a late
seventeenth-century baroque
royal garden whose effects
were achieved by ground
pattern, enclosure and rigid
symmetry. The early
eighteenth-century groundplan
by Christiaan Pieter van Staden
(*opposite*) records its two phases
of development. The area as
far as the cross-axis canal was
the extent of the garden before
1688 and the area beyond it
was added after William
became King of England, when
it was deliberately extended to
reflect his new regal status.

THE VIEW FROM THE ROOF OF
Het Loo (*above*) looks down on
the main axis towards the
central fountain of Venus
flanked by parterres composed
of clipped grass and box set
against various coloured
grounds. Such elaborate display
beds were placed next to the
house to be viewed from the
first floor windows. A detail
(*left*) of the re-created parterre
in the Queen's Garden shows
these elements even more
clearly: clipped box against
three shades of gravel or stone
chippings and the enclosing
flower border, known as a
plate bande, itself enclosed by
box hedging, in which flowers
were planted at intervals like
botanic specimens.

23

to have flowers in all seasons in order to make two or three bouquets, bound in ribbon for the service of her Highness every week'. William, for his part, swept away what were by then the old-fashioned circles of hornbeam at the back of the house and replaced them with a *parterre de broderie*. He also turned his attention to the fountains, a garden feature for which he would have a lifelong obsession. Honselaarsdijk anticipated Het Loo, the couple's greatest Dutch garden, and the aristocrat in charge of running William's gardens, Hans Willem Bentinck, was to cross to England and head the team that planted Hampton Court. Indeed Honselaarsdijk was to be the chief source of bulbs and flowers at Hampton Court throughout the 1690s.

Bentinck, a close friend of William's, had been used by William in all his negotiations with England, including the ones for his marriage to Mary and those which led up to the events of 1688. He himself owned one of the most spectacular gardens of the age at Zorgvliet, which included an impressive orangery housing one of the best collections of exotic plants in the Netherlands. Once in England he would make another remarkable garden at Bulstrode in Buckinghamshire and was to remain the King's right-hand man in all his garden projects.

Work began on the new palace of Het Loo in April 1685 and was to go in two phases. The initial phase was under the direction of the Dutch architect, Jacob Roman, with the close involvement of Bentinck. During the second phase, on William's accession to the British throne in 1689, both palace and garden were enlarged to reflect the enhanced position of its owner. In this 'work of prodigious expense, infinite variety and curiosity', as Het Loo was described at the time, the designer Daniel Marot clearly contributed to the splendid interior decoration and the design of the garden parterres, although he was not privy to the initial planning and lay-out.

Marot was a Huguenot who had fled France soon after the Revocation of the Edict of Nantes in 1685 and settled in the Low Countries. A designer in the broadest sense of the word, he covered both interior decoration and every aspect of garden design from parterres to fountains, and in this he was unlike André Mollet or George London but a precursor of William Kent in the next century. As a result his work was distinguished by the close integration of interior and exterior, the same pattern, for instance, being used for the embroidery on bed hangings and in a *parterre de broderie*. His chief role, however, was to adapt the style of Louis XIV's court for countries whose traditions were far different. In the garden he was a major innovator, using bold rhythmic arabesque designs for hedges, parterres and formal copses so that they reached a pitch of elaboration unseen before.

Marot's masterpiece was to be Hampton Court and Het Loo, in which he had a hand, can be regarded as a trial run for that far grander project. Het Loo, as made for William and Mary when reigning British monarchs, was in miniature a baroque palace of a kind the earlier Stuarts never achieved. Its importance to William is evident in his plea to Bentinck, whom he sent to Holland in the winter of 1688–89 to check on the state of the gardens: 'Do not forget Het Loo,' he wrote, 'nor to go there and sort out what remains to be done; you know how that place is close to my heart.' Bentinck did not forget and went on to check another of the royal gardens at Dieren where, finding that a drunken gardener had flooded the maze, he fired him.

At Het Loo house and garden achieve a total unity through the strong north-south central axis which cuts straight through the forecourt, house and garden and is extended both ways into the surrounding landscape. On either side the interior rooms and exterior garden 'rooms' form symmetrical mirror images. This unity of inside and out was furthered by Marot's attention to the slightest detail. Thus the vases in the garden appear, flower-bedecked, on the painted ceilings and the bold rhythmic arabesques of the ironwork doors find their counterpart in the patterns made by the box in the parterres. Brick, stone, wood, iron, glass, gravel, trees, shrubs, flowers and above all water were orchestrated into a total visual harmony, paying tribute to their owner who now ruled four kingdoms.

Moreover, the visitor was exposed not only to an overwhelming visual and aural experience, in the contrast between the wild terrain outside and the ordered splendour inside the walls, and in the exotic plants, the superb sculpture and the amazing water effects but also one which engaged the intellect. For the garden was meant to be read as royal visual propaganda, which the King called on the Dutch artist Romeyn de Hooghe to devise. The sculptured recumbent river-gods from whose urns flow the waters which feed the garden's fountains are of deities of rivers within William's rule. Mary figures in the central fountain as Venus, goddess of love and of gardens, while the fountain of the infant Hercules strangling the serpent symbolized William's

THE VISTA ALONG THE MAIN AXIS AT HET LOO (*opposite above*) encapsulates the importance attached to spectacular water effects as manifestations of regal magnificence. The first fountain is dedicated to Venus, goddess of love and of gardens, born from the sea and so supported by gilded tritons, who also represented the Queen. In the distance the King's fountain, with its enormously high central jet, celebrates his power as well as the hydraulic skills of his engineers.

THE CASCADES AT HET LOO, SEEN IN A CONTEMPORARY ENGRAVING BY Romeyn de Hooghe and re-created today (*opposite below*), include elements essential to any baroque palace garden. The contrast between the immaculately ordered garden and the wild wood beyond its confines is emphasized by an elegant raised terrace on which courtiers could stroll or sit to admire the patterns of the garden below and by the elaborate wooden trellis work. Originally the central figure represented Arion playing his lyre, a character from classical mythology who was thrown overboard and rescued, thanks to his melodious music-making, by a dolphin; in the same way William III was to be viewed as taming his subjects by the harmony of his rule.

PREVIOUS PAGE: THE PANORAMIC PAINTING OF HAMPTON COURT BY
Leonard Knyff captures the gardens at their height shortly before
William III's death in 1702. Beneath the east façade of the palace
stretches the vast semicircular Fountain Garden; the outer ring is made
up of parterres of turf cut into patterns outlined with box hedges; the
inner two beds are parterres of box set against coloured gravels.
Dotted inside the parterres are the statues which now stand in the
East Terrace Garden at Windsor Castle. At either end of the central
walk are superb urns: two are still there today, two others are now
preserved in the Orangery at Kensington Palace.
Along the north side of the palace, behind the Tudor tennis court, are
the kitchen gardens and, beyond them, the so-called wilderness. This
consisted of walks and compartments enclosed by clipped hedges and
included the maze which still exists in the far north-west corner.
To the south, on the site of the first Tudor gardens, there is a series of
small gardens: the King's Privy Garden in its final form, the largest, is
contained at the river end by Tijou's ironwork screens and surrounded
by raised walks on one of which is Queen Mary's Arbour; beyond are
an orchard, a rectangular site now called the Pond Garden, and the
areas in which Queen Mary had her orangery, flower gardens and hot-
houses. Near the river is the Tudor-style banqueting house with its
adjacent *volière* or bird garden.

THE AERIAL VIEW OF HAMPTON COURT TODAY
(*above*) shows how much of basic late seventeenth-century garden
structure is still intact.

heroic struggles against the French King, Louis XIV. Even the
plants could be symbolic: the rare orange trees in tubs brought
out to adorn the Queen's garden each summer were emblems
of her husband's family, the House of Orange, and the flowers
planted in the King's garden could be in his colours of orange
and blue. The superb stone urns on the terrace, designed by
Marot, celebrated both the King's virtues and his kingdoms.

Everywhere the visitor looked he was meant to respond to
nature perfected in the reign of a golden age ruler. Even the
advanced hydraulic engineering, which produced the astounding
vertical jet of water of the greatest fountain, was seen as a
tribute to the power and prestige of such a sovereign.

Nor was the Queen neglected. Her garden was planted with
flowers that were considered feminine, such as columbines and
lilies, and here too she had her collection of exotics, which in
winter were housed in an orangery and in the service wing of
the palace. The man in charge was Daniel Desmarets, who had
been appointed 'Intendant of His Highness's Country Houses,
Plantations and Gardens' in 1685. An inventory of 1713 lists no
less than 213 exotic plants at Het Loo, including a pomegranate,
a myrtle, a fig and an oleander, all rare collector's items.

Such palace gardens as Het Loo were designed primarily as
expressions of princely magnificence. The numerous engravings
produced of the Het Loo garden were all part of a propaganda
programme that aimed to present William III as a monarch who
could eclipse *le roi soleil*, his rival Louis XIV. And that desire of
William's was the driving force behind his greatest creation,
Hampton Court.

There were two major phases in the development of the
Hampton Court gardens, the first from 1689 to 1694, when
Mary died, and the second from 1699 until William's death in
1702, a phase prompted by the destruction by fire of Whitehall
Palace. The choice of Hampton Court as the couple's main
palace was partly determined by the King's asthma and his need
to avoid the polluted air of the metropolis, but it was also
because the flat terrain and the Long Water evoked William's
beloved homeland.

From the outset both King and Queen took a deep personal
interest in every aspect of the new palace, which was the work
of Sir Christopher Wren, and even more of the garden. Daniel
Defoe perhaps exaggerated when he wrote that the garden was
'devised by the King himself' but certainly 'the amendments and
alterations were made by the King, or the Queen's special com-
mand, or both, for their Majesties agreed so well in their fancy,
and both had so good a judgement in the just proportion of
things, in which are the principal beauties of a garden, that it
may be said that they both ordered everything that was done'.

For this task William formed what might be called a garden
cabinet. Following his accession in 1689, he rewarded his friend
Bentinck with the title of Earl of Portland and appointed him
Superintendent of the King's Gardens. At the same time George
London was appointed Portland's Deputy in controlling the

creation and maintenance (but not the design) of the royal gardens. London, who has already appeared in the story of Charles II's gardens, had worked for Henry Compton, Bishop of London, who had been responsible for the religious education of Mary and her sister Anne. Compton had been one of the revolutionary committee who had invited William to invade and when he first met the King he had taken London with him.

By this time London had already laid out two of the most famous new gardens in England, Longleat for Lord Weymouth and Burghley for Lord Exeter, and had just begun Chatsworth, his masterpiece. He was in charge of the Brompton Park Nursery, about to be joined by Henry Wise, and under him the nursery was to dominate English garden design for decades, thanks to his remarkable energy and social connections. A friend of London, the architect William Talman, received the post of Comptroller under Portland and would provide the architecture London needed for his long series of country house gardens. Together, these three men formed the official structure responsible for the English royal gardens, with Daniel Marot joining them as the designer outsider at the behest of the King.

The initial phase of work at Hampton Court began immediately, with the making of the Great Parterre or the Fountain Garden, while in the park the existing avenue flanking the Long Water was complemented by two more avenues. One looked from the Queen's study towards Kingston church and a second, mirroring it on the other side, provided a vista to Thames Ditton. All three avenues culminated in the new east façade of the palace and, as at Het Loo, the central axis was to be sacrosanct. Beneath this façade was laid out the greatest parterre ever made in late seventeenth-century England, one with a most unusual shape, a semicircle, for it filled the area made by the arc of lime trees planted under Charles II.

Daniel Marot's design for this stupendous parterre is dated August 1689 and follows that of Het Loo: a terrace, this time a wide and long gravel walk, which was to have been divided from the garden by a series of railings and gates. These were commissioned from the great Huguenot metalworker, Jean Tijou, but were so long in the making that by the time they arrived it was decided to place them elsewhere. Another change was to Marot's design for one huge turf parterre in complex patterns, set against gravels and vertically offset by topiary. Instead, the two beds nearest the palace became *parterres de broderie* with flowing scrollwork patterns in box hedging. The six parterres surrounding them were created according to the design in turf and were held in by a raised lime walk where people could stroll and look down on the patterns. All of this was contained within a semicircle of railings punctuated by two magnificent gates by Tijou which led out into the avenues.

To add to this splendour there were initially to be no less than eleven fountains with a huge oval one on the central axis. The King took a particularly close personal interest, as Defoe recorded, in 'the dimensions of the fountains, and what quantity

THE MAZE OF HEDGES AT HAMPTON COURT IS THE ONLY PART OF THE original seventeenth-century wilderness which survives today.

of water they should cast up, and increased the number of them after the first design'. In Knyff's painting, there are indeed thirteen not eleven fountains, although sadly they were never to operate properly.

Work began simultaneously on the wilderness, of which a small section, albeit replanted, exists today: the famous maze. Wildernesses, despite the modern connotations, were in fact formal enclosed areas intersected by patterns of paths making walks and 'rooms' delineated by hedges. Within the 'rooms' there would be arbours and seats and fragrant flowering shrubs. André Mollet had planted a small one for Henrietta Maria at Wimbledon but the Hampton Court wilderness was on a scale to make it one of the wonders of the age; its area was equal to that occupied by the entire palace today.

Virtually for certain designed by Marot, in plan the paths formed a St Andrew's cross with a rectangle superimposed on it and within that a symmetrical arrangement of curves which in style looked forward from the baroque to the rococo. The paths were flanked by hornbeam hedges tall enough to conceal any sight of the old Tudor palace, which was deemed to be 'offensive', and the garden 'rooms' thus formed were filled with trees, shrubs and climbing plants. In addition to the surviving hedged maze there was a second, flat one of turf with gravel paths. In the centre of the wilderness there was a large pine tree and specimen trees were dotted through the composition, acting as vertical accents. This mysterious enclosure could be used by members of the court for the important exercise of walking, as well as for religious meditation.

The following year, 1690, a new Privy Garden was laid out for the King in answer to Wren's new façade on the south side which incorporated, at ground level, an orangery and a grotto. An engraving shows that this lost garden was a comparatively simple turf parterre, rectangular and divided into quarters, with raised terraces on either side. On one of these was the *berceau* or tunnel arbour, one of the ancestors of today's pergolas, known as Queen Mary's Arbour, which is still there in replanted form today; but a handsome circular ironwork structure, rather like a gazebo, decorated on the inside by the French painter Louis Laguerre, has long since vanished. The garden also included the first major sculptural commissions: two magnificent vases, one by Caius Gabriel Cibber depicting the Triumph of Bacchus and the other, by Edward Pierce, of Amphytrite and Nereids. Pierce had worked extensively with Wren on the rebuilt City churches, while Cibber was to become 'sculptor in ordinary unto His Majesty' in 1697. The culmination of the garden's vista was a fountain by Hubert Le Sueur made in the 1630s, which had been moved to Hampton Court by Cromwell and was given a new pedestal by Pierce.

Dutch gardeners were brought over to lay out and maintain this and the other gardens at Hampton Court, which had a Netherlandish input at every level. Hendrik Quellenburg came from Honselaarsdijk to be head gardener in the Privy Garden,

Samuel van Staden in the wilderness and Caspar Gamperle in the hot-houses. Mary had brought from Holland her plant collection, which by 1690 included 'about 400 rare Indian plants which were never seen in England'. These were housed in her celebrated glasshouses, which rested against a brick wall with stoves behind it and extended five feet from the wall at the top and eight at the bottom.

These hot-houses had been erected as early as April 1689 in the area further along the south façade on the site of the original Tudor gardens which were now the domain of the Queen. While the new palace was being built, she lived in what was known as the Water Gallery, a lavishly decorated pavilion filled with her collection of blue and white delftware, and from which she was able to direct operations in the series of smaller gardens over which she presided and which might almost be categorized as a series of botanical gardens. In one area seeds were germinated and in the last years of her life ones from the East Indies, the Cape and Barbados were planted. A second section was devoted to displaying auriculas, cult plants of the age whose every variation of colouring and marking was studied and admired. These were brought out in containers and arranged on shelves like an exhibition. A final area was given over to flowers, again planted like specimens for study.

Although Mary's botanical collection never led the field (there were other more important collections), she and her husband shared to the full the late seventeenth-century passion for exotic plants. It stemmed from partly scientific or medicinal reasons but such plants were also for purposes of prestige. However splendid the formal gardens at Hampton Court, a collection of very rare plants was an even more exalted status symbol. In

1691 Mary appointed Leonard Plunkenet Queen's Botanist to assist her in forming the collection. Plunkenet's major work, *Phytographia*, which Linnaeus described as an *opus incomparabile*, ran into three parts, dedicated to Bishop Compton, Portland and the King respectively, and included 2740 pictures of plants.

Mary died of smallpox in 1694 and as Stephen Switzer, the garden designer and writer, later wrote, 'Upon the death of that illustrious Princess, gardening and all other pleasures were under eclipse with that Prince.' William was deeply affected by the loss and it was not until five years later, prompted by the burning of Whitehall, that there was a fresh burst of gardening activity at Hampton Court. It was, however, to be on a scale equalling the first phase and the amounts spent in each case were in excess of £40,000.

Work suddenly began again on the Fountain Garden and in 1700 the plumber connected up the pipes so that the King could see 'experiments of several jed'eau's and jets of water'. A new sculptor, Jan van Nost, prepared a model for the great central fountain, 'with 4 shells, 4 dolphins, one sea-horse and 11 other figures', although the statuary was never to be made. More important was the addition of sculpture to the parterres. Hubert Le Sueur's classical statues of Diana, Hercules and Apollo, made for Charles I, were moved here from the garden at St James's, along with his cast of the Borghese Warrior, which was taken from the head of the canal in St James's Park where it had been placed by Charles II. Provided with new pedestals by van Nost, they were symmetrically arranged through the parterres. Two superb urns flanked the Long Water: these splendid pieces, one by Pierce depicting Meleager hunting the Calydonian Boar and the other by Cibber of the Judgement of Paris, are now in the

Orangery at Kensington. They may have begun their life in the King's Privy Garden and, like the same sculptors' two vases that began on the terrace there, been moved to the Fountain Garden, where the vases remain to this day.

The Privy Garden, which was extended south to the Thames, underwent the most dramatic transformation of all. The Tijou ironwork screens, commissioned in 1693 for the Fountain Garden, were arranged here to provide a dazzling finale at the far end of the garden. A statue of Apollo was set up on a circle of grass in front of the screens as a focal point in 1702, the year of the King's death. In the centre of the garden there was a large fountain with a single jet, around which stretched an elegant turf parterre in scrolling patterns that suggest the work of Marot. No less than eight hundred clipped yews and hollies were part of the composition, which was enhanced in the summer months by the symmetrical placing of tubs containing orange trees. Some of the hollies, once clipped pyramids about six feet high, are still identifiable today, although they have now grown to a height of twenty to thirty feet.

As well as all this, Mary's Water Gallery was demolished and a banqueting house erected which looked almost Tudor on the outside but inside was adorned with baroque illusionistic painting. Even within the palace a garden was laid out in the Fountain Court with a statue of Diana by Fanelli as its focal point, surrounded by topiary pyramids and globes. But the most significant decision was to create a new major approach to the palace from the north across Bushy Park. A vast avenue costing over £4000 was planted, consisting of four rows of lime trees and one of chestnut. It was to be punctuated by a pond with a 400-foot diameter, for the middle of which van Nost designed a

WILLIAM III'S FIRST PRIVY GARDEN (*left*), depicted by Sutton Nicholls in *c*.1696, was laid out on the site of Henry VIII's to complement the new façade of the palace. The garden was flanked by raised terraces looking down on to a parterre of green turf cut into patterns.

The central path led to a fountain surmounted by a statue of the nymph Arethusa by Hubert Le Sueur, made originally for Queen Henrietta Maria, Charles II's mother, for her garden at Somerset House.

THE ARETHUSA FOUNTAIN, discarded when William enlarged the Privy Garden, was placed by his sister-in-law, Queen Anne, in the centre of the pond in Bushy Park (*left*) where it still remains. The pond was part of William's grandiose scheme for a new approach to Hampton Court which was never finished.

statue of the King. William's death left this bold avenue uncompleted; the pond must have been far advanced, for it is still there today, but Anne would cancel the statue, substituting the redundant Arethusa from the old Privy Garden.

Beside the glory of Hampton Court, the other English garden created by William and Mary, at Kensington, could not compete. But Kensington was never intended as a major palace, only as a private retreat where the King could quickly escape from the damp atmosphere of Whitehall, for Kensington was then a village away from the London fogs. William and Mary had purchased what was then Nottingham House from Daniel Finch, 2nd Earl of Nottingham, for £14,000 in 1689 and promptly showed their love of gardens by creating an intimate Dutch-style garden. There were seventeen acres of formal garden stretching away from the south front, with the Queen's Privy Garden to the east, and by 1696 no less than forty staff were required to maintain these gardens, headed by another Dutchman, Heinrich Timmerman.

William and Mary's garden at Kensington no longer exists and the visual evidence of what it looked like is contradictory. However, a groundplan of 1715 matches an engraving of about the same date in showing a geometrical design that suggests the hand of Marot. Turf parterres stand near the palace and a wilderness with *bosquets*, formally planted copses, beyond them. What at first glance seems to be a central-axis path flanked, as at Het Loo and Hampton Court, with mirror-image patterns, turns out not to be so. In a highly ingenious solution to an asymmetrical area, the central walk is focussed on the main façade but is not in fact truly central and the spaces on either side are not the same width or shape. This decision by Marot – if indeed it be he – to vary the patterns on either side anticipates the breakdown of formality which was to come. It must have been a very unusual garden experience, for unlike that at Hampton Court, the woodland area with its hedged walks and 'rooms' almost grows out of the formal flatter areas near the palace.

In the last few years of William's life, at the same time as new work was going ahead at Hampton Court, he also had gardening ambitions for Windsor Castle and Greenwich. The King's lifelong rival, Louis XIV, had finally had to agree to military peace and in the aftermath of the 1697 Treaty of Rijswijk, Portland was sent as ambassador to Versailles, taking with

him the Royal Gardener, George London. Portland was under instructions to study the great masterpieces of Le Nôtre and, if possible, to persuade him to come to England. The sharp horticultural competition between the two kings is clear in a letter from Portland to William in February 1698 in which he reports that although the orange trees at Versailles are 'extremely beautiful, and large and numerous' their heads are not as good as those at Honselaarsdijk. And, administering a final *coup de grâce* to the Sun King's gardens, there were no flowers in any of the gardens, 'not even a snowdrop'.

Portland and London failed to bring Le Nôtre to England but they arrived back in 1698 with his nephew, Claude Desgotz. The King wanted him to design lay-outs for both Windsor Castle and Greenwich. Drawings for both survive and although the Greenwich design seems to have remained strictly on paper, work at Windsor was begun. In July 1698 William 'viewed the ground around about the castle marked out by Mr London and the director of the French king's gardens, who came over with the earl of Portland'. The following year the steep slope on the north side began to be terraced and work started on digging the canal which appears in the Desgotz design.

All of this was, however, to be as dust when on 20 February 1702 the King's horse tripped on a molehill in Hampton Court park, throwing him to the ground. On 8 March he died. He and Mary had, however, triggered a phenomenal *furor hortensis* from the time of their arrival in England and as Daniel Defoe wrote, 'with the particular judgement of the king, all the gentlemen in England began to fall in; and in a few years, fine gardens . . . began to grow up in every corner; the king began with the gardens of Hampton Court and Kensington, and the gentlemen followed everywhere, with such a gust that the alteration is indeed wonderful throughout the kingdom'.

On William's death, however, the royal gardens were to undergo a clean sweep, made the more thorough by the new Queen's intense dislike of her brother-in-law. Anne alluded to William as Caliban, and she had little more affection for her sister, to whom she had refused even a deathbed reconciliation. She came to the throne at the age of thirty-seven, uneducated and untrained for rulership, though her reign was to see England's great military victories under Marlborough.

Anne had been married in 1683 to George, Prince of Denmark, a dull man who suffered, like William, from asthma all his life and together they presided over a dull court. Her health had been ruined by seventeen unfruitful pregnancies, and she was now also riddled with gout. But she was still a Stuart, with a passionate if erratic belief in the divinity of kings. And she loved gardens. When her only surviving son died aged twelve, she was 'daily carried in her chair in to the garden, to divert her melancholy thoughts'.

A MONOGRAM OF WILLIAM AND MARY ON A KEYSTONE ON THE Privy Garden façade of Hampton Court (*above*).

WHAT IS NOW CALLED THE POND GARDEN AT HAMPTON COURT (*left*), after the Tudor garden which occupied exactly the same area, was one of Mary II's flower gardens.

Two months after William's death she wrote to her friend, Sarah, the future Duchess of Marlborough: 'I went to Kensington to walk in the garden, which would be a very pretty place if it were well kept, but nothing could be worse. It is a great pity that there should be no better use made of so great an allowance, for I have been told the king allowed £400 a year for the one garden.'

Anne's approach to her garden inheritance was inconsistent. Part of it seems conditioned by an almost vindictive cost-cutting exercise motivated by her loathing of her brother-in-law. Another part, however, was to be benevolent, and she was to spend lavishly on Kensington. When she went to a meeting of the Lords of the Treasury in order 'to restrain the expense of the gardens', George London unfortunately chose the occasion to petition for arrears owed to the gardeners. He came away not only without the arrears but also minus his job. Henry Wise was summoned to the next meeting and told the Lords that he could maintain the royal gardens for £1600 instead of £4800. He was appointed Royal Gardener as from 1 August 1702, and he was to hold office until he retired in 1727.

The Queen spent the winter months at St James's and Kensington, with a preference for the latter, and the summer at Hampton Court and Windsor Castle. Financial constraints seem very much to have dictated what was done. St James's was left virtually as Mollet planted it. At Windsor the terracing and canal under construction were much simplified and any attempt to elaborate and create a wilderness was sabotaged by flood water from the Thames. At Hampton Court the activities were similarly negative. A London merchant who had sold the late King £555 worth of Italian statuary was told in no uncertain terms that 'he may have the statues again'. When the effects of van Nost's studio were sold, the pieces clearly destined for Hampton Court, including the statue of William, were among them; and Tijou's petition for £1889 of work expenses was rejected.

More sadly, the desecration of Marot's masterpiece began. In 1703 Anne had a scheme prepared to alter the Fountain Garden at Hampton Court. It was rejected on the grounds of expense but by 1708 a major transformation had taken place. An undated plan by Henry Wise shows the type of dramatic simplification that had been proposed. All the fountains except the central one were swept away. The great *parterre de broderie* vanished; all of the box hedging – Anne disliked the smell of box – and the elaborate cut turf-work were banished in favour of simpler areas of plain grass edged with *plates bandes*, narrow beds which contained clipped evergreens and flowers.

Within a few years the greatest baroque garden ever made in this country was decimated. Anne's husband had at least commissioned Leonard Knyff to make a series of drawings of the gardens before the hand of destruction fell. These provide a unique record of the Hampton Court garden at its apogee, although Knyff was left, along with many of the Queen's creditors, lamenting in January 1702 about 'not being payd for them'.

At Kensington Palace, Anne's first works, wrote Stephen Switzer, 'were the rooting up the box and giving an English model to the old-made gardens'. An engraving shows what these gardens looked like in her reign, although it is not known how far she changed them. The Queen's only certain addition was Wren's monumental garden seat, built for her in 1706–7. The work was not cheap. Over £400 was spent on the seat by April 1705 and the following year a mason received over £550 for further work on it.

Anne's greatest creation, however, was a thirty-acre wilderness to the north of the palace. Although work on a wilderness had begun under William, it now continued unabated and this area of geometric shady walks included one of Wise's masterpieces: a sunken garden with six shallow terraces made from an old gravel pit. This was a great novelty and drew applause from no less a person than Addison: 'It must have been a fine genius for gardening that could have thought of forming such an unsightly hollow into so beautiful an area and to have hit the eye with so uncommon and agreeable a scene as that which it is now wrought into.'

The amounts of money lavished by Anne on that were huge but nothing compared with what she spent on building work in the garden, above all on what became known as the Orangery. The first estimate, in June 1704, was £2599 5s 1d but a month later Hawksmoor's plan was revised by Vanbrugh and by the time that the building was completed in 1705 it had cost over £6000. It must rank as the most splendid orangery of the period and also a monument to the side of Anne that embodied garden prodigality as against parsimony. It was also a perfect expression of its age when the garden banqueting house of earlier periods was giving way to the Orangery, in reality a glass-fronted garden room not just for wintering plants but to use in the summer months for social purposes.

The favourable press Anne's gardens were given by contemporary and near contemporary garden writers was in sharp contrast to that given William III's gardens. The reaction against 'Dutch William' was immediate and strong, and the attack on his garden style was more an attack on him. Anne's so-called reform of his gardens was presented in a patriotic light as a reassertion of the English style that had been perverted by an imported foreign one. Switzer, in 1745, wrote of 'pleasure gardens being stuffed thick with box, a fashion brought over out of Holland by the Dutch gardeners, who used it to a fault'. He referred to topiary as 'the *Dutch* taste, which came in with the revolution', although in fact box parterres went back to the 1630s and topiary to the Tudor period.

With the advent of the landscape style later in the century the garden style of William and Mary was soon to be viewed as pure anathema. And yet in the history of the royal gardens, the reign of William and Mary could be seen as their finest hour. Nothing either before or since matches the spectacular glory of this couple's gardens.

THE FORMAL GARDEN
(*above*), stretching south of
Kensington Palace, was begun
in the 1690s by William and
Mary and continued and
expanded by Anne. In this
engraving of the garden of
c.1715, patterns in turf and
small trees near the palace give
way to areas of trees and
shrubs intricately laid out to
create curving paths and
'rooms'. The kitchen gardens
lie to the north-west of the
palace, while the area to the
east is parkland used for
hunting. Nothing remains of
this garden today except the
main path, and also Queen
Anne's Orangery which can be
seen here to the north east of
the palace.

THE GARDEN ALCOVE
(*left*), designed for Queen Anne
by Wren in 1706–7, was an
enormously expensive feature.
It was originally placed at the
end of the central avenue of
the garden to the south of
Kensington Palace, where it
can be seen from the back in
the engraving above. Today it
stands in the north of
Kensington Gardens, near
Lancaster Gate.

GARDENS OF THE MIND

QUEEN CAROLINE, WIFE OF GEORGE II

Caroline of Ansbach (1683–1737), who married the future George II in 1705, was the first of three German princesses who were to dominate royal garden-making in England through the eighteenth century. An extraordinary woman, masculine in character and of ample Teutonic build with a fresh complexion, blue eyes and flaxen hair, Caroline was to put the royal gardens in the forefront of every development during a period unprecedented for its ferment of new ideas as to what constituted a garden. Suddenly England, up till then on the periphery of garden innovation, became its leader with the new revolutionary style known as the landscape movement. It was to sweep away the grand formal gardens of the previous century not only in Britain but also, to a large extent, on the continental mainland.

The daughter of a minor German Protestant prince, Caroline was only three when her father died and she and her mother moved to the court of the future King and Queen of Prussia, then Elector and Electress of Brandenburg. At the age of twelve her mother also died and Caroline became an orphan, but at one of the most intellectually brilliant courts in Europe.

CAROLINE IN 1716 WHEN PRINCESS OF WALES; A DETAIL OF A PORTRAIT BY Sir Godfrey Kneller. The German-born Princess expressed her identity as Queen of Great Britain by adopting wholeheartedly the revolutionary new English landscape style of gardening.

THE SERPENTINE IN KENSINGTON GARDENS IS ONE OF THE MASTERPIECES OF ornamental water to survive from the eighteenth century. Created between 1730 and 1731 out of ten separate ponds, it was revolutionary in breaking away from the fashion for formal geometric pools. Today its originality and importance are largely forgotten; a busy road bisects the stretch of water on which the royal family once sailed in two yachts and which is now the haunt of swimmers and small pleasure boats.

Under the leadership of the Electress, Sophie Charlotte, the Charlottenburg palace in Berlin became a centre for philosophers and men of learning. Her influence on her young ward was to be decisive, forming Caroline into Britain's last truly intellectual queen and also passing on to her a passion for garden-making, for it was from 1695 onwards, during Caroline's most formative years, that the Electress had the gardens of the palace laid out. Sophie Charlotte consulted her cousin, Elisabeth-Charlotte of Orléans, Louis XIV's sister-in-law, who lived amidst the garden of St Cloud, one of the masterpieces of Le Nôtre. A French designer was sent to Brandenburg and his plans were submitted to the aged Le Nôtre for approval. The result was a garden in the French style of the highest order, one which was to have a huge influence in Germany.

Sophie Charlotte died in 1705, the year in which Caroline was married to the future George II, then heir to the Elector of Hanover. George, in sharp contrast to his wife, loved the chase, loathed men of letters, books, painting and poetry, and would dismiss her obsession with garden-making as 'childish silly stuff'. He none the less remained devoted to her, and respected her cleverness, although this did not hinder him from taking mistresses. The marriage took Caroline to a second court and a second famous garden but of an earlier date, Herrenhausen, which had been created during the 1680s under the aegis of another remarkable woman, the Electress Sophia. She had sent her gardener to Holland for its design and the baroque garden, which still survives, is not unlike Het Loo and Hampton Court with its progression from elaborate parterres to geometrical *bosquets*, the entire enclosure held in by canals. Sophia, a woman of great physical stamina, would exhaust her entourage walking up and down the allées at Herrenhausen for up to three hours without stopping, a custom which Caroline was to follow.

As the last surviving child of James I's daughter, Elizabeth, Queen of Bohemia, Sophia was the dynastic link whereby the House of Hanover would succeed that of Stuart on the death of Queen Anne in 1714. She died only a few months before Anne, at the enormous age of eighty-four, thus just missing becoming Queen of Britain. Instead, her son succeeded as George I and Caroline came to England with her husband, as the Prince and Princess of Wales.

The pair brought with them from Hanover what was to be a *leitmotif* in royal family history until the accession of George IV in 1820: each ruler was to hate his heir. This was to have not only political but also cultural consequences. By 1717 George I and his son were not on speaking terms and the Prince and Princess of Wales, banished from the royal palaces, acquired Leicester House as their London residence, followed two years later by Richmond Lodge for use during the summer months. However, devoid of any substantial income, Caroline could do nothing in the way of garden-making until 1727, when George I died and her husband became king.

Caroline adored splendour and cultivated power. On finding herself queen, she quickly created around her a court which was to be the antithesis of that of her father-in-law. Her ladies-in-waiting were both beauties and women of strong character and intellect, and to her circle were bidden the leading writers of the age. She had a deep interest in theology and in Newtonian science, and she equally patronized the visual arts. Horace Walpole unkindly characterized her as having 'great pretensions to learning and taste, with not much of the former and none of the latter'.

Through her alliance with the prime minister, Sir Robert Walpole, Caroline manipulated the political will of the King and her power became more substantive because she acted as Regent on no less than four occasions during her husband's absence in Hanover. More pertinently, her alliance with Walpole ensured that Parliament voted her the largest annual allowance ever bestowed on a queen consort, £100,000. And this was to pay for the royal garden renaissance she inaugurated.

George I had been quite content to live in the surroundings that he had inherited from his Stuart predecessors and only during the last year of his life did he embark on a huge garden project at Kensington. In 1705 a hundred acres of Hyde Park to the east had been acquired to form a paddock for the royal deer and antelope. This George I decided to transform to accommodate not only them but his extensive menagerie, which included tigers and civet cats. Cages were needed, plus a large pond for the turtles, and the public was to be excluded by a nine-foot-high wall enclosing what was called the Royal Paddock.

This now forms the major part of what we know today as Kensington Gardens, a miraculous survival in central London of a great formal planting of the early eighteenth century. Its history is, however, confused, for the work was carried out over two to three years during which not only the monarch changed but also the officers in charge of royal garden-making. The scheme was under way during the tenure of George I's 'Surveyor of Gardens and Waters', the architect Sir John Vanbrugh, who died in March 1726. The landscape designer, Charles Bridgeman, was brought in six months later while George I was still on the throne. Then, after the King's death in June 1727, Caroline took over the project, working with Bridgeman.

Kensington Gardens thus involves the work of two men, both of whom are major figures on the pathway leading to 'Capability' Brown and a totally new gardening approach. Although Vanbrugh is not known to have ever designed a garden, he is considered to be the most important stimulus to gardening imagination during the first quarter of the eighteenth century. Before he entered royal service in 1715 he had been intricately involved in two of the grandest of all gardening projects, at Castle Howard and Blenheim Palace. Although at Kensington Gardens he was still working in the old formal style, he was already a major pioneer of the new attitudes, whose essence is contained in his recommendation, albeit ignored, to the Duchess of Marlborough. Vanbrugh advised her to retain the ancient royal manor of Woodstock because it was 'One of the Most Agreeable Objects that the best Landskip Painters can invent' and conducive to 'lively and pleasing Reflections'.

This new attitude was, however, hardly in evidence in the initial plan for Kensington Gardens, which is decidedly backward-looking. The elderly Henry Wise was still Royal Gardener, in charge of the maintenance of all the royal gardens, and the King himself, whose tastes were nothing if not conservative, is known to have taken an active interest in the lay-out. The avenues and trees were laid out, it was recorded, 'by His Majesty's own direction' and the arrangement largely reworks the formula of Hampton Court.

Planting had already begun in September 1726, before Bridgeman arrived, and it is likely that he spent his initial period carrying out an inherited design. All of this changed after the old King's death in the following year, when Bridgeman and Caroline set out to modify the formal scheme.

Caroline's education had exposed her to the influence of two innovative garden-making consorts and now with Bridgeman, and later Kent, she was prepared to make the leap from formality and to embrace a revolution rather than a development in garden design.

Bridgeman was a man of humble origins who seems to have begun his career in the famous Brompton Park Nursery and even before 1714 was collaborating with Henry Wise. They became partners in 1726, acting jointly for a short time as Chief Gardeners caring for the 148 acres of royal gardens around five palaces. When in March 1728 Wise, then in his seventies, finally retired, Bridgeman was appointed Royal Gardener. By then he was an established and respected figure in the world of the arts and polite society, laying out gardens for the leading Whig aristocracy: he had already embarked on his masterpiece and the most famous garden of the eighteenth century, Lord Cobham's grounds at Stowe. Sir Robert Walpole was certainly a patron and he could easily have dropped Bridgeman's name into the ear of the Queen. Nor would he have lacked support from the King, for Bridgeman had advised the royal mistress, Henrietta Howard, on the lay-out of her grounds at Marble Hill.

Bridgeman was a pioneer of the so-called *jardin anglais* and his work forms the vital link between the geometric lay-outs of the 1700s and the freer style of 'Capability' Brown in the 1750s and 1760s. It is an intermediary phase which might in modern stylistic terms be called rococo and it stemmed from a radically different view of the role of a garden, even a royal one. Anti-French and fiercely patriotic, it aimed to realize in the English landscape the classical elysiums described by Ovid, Virgil and Pliny the Younger. Joseph Addison summed up the new Augustan ideals in two garden visions: one set out to create 'delightful Landskips . . . made out of Fields and Woods, Herds of Cattle, and Swarms of Bees', the other was composed of glades of trees among which were scattered temples, ruins, 'marble trophies, carved pillars, and statues of lawgivers, heroes, statesmen, philo-

sophers and poets'. It was picture painting with the countryside as the canvas and trees and plants, water, buildings and sculpture as the paint. These garden 'pictures' were meant to be read by the onlooker and provided the vehicles whereby owners might exhibit their taste in letters, painting, poetry and architecture, their knowledge of classical antiquity, their political affiliations, their pride in ownership and cultivation of rural life as an ideal of civilized living.

Such a style also set off to advantage the new trees and shrubs which arrived in England through the century from America and Europe. There were, for example, species of birch, rhododendrons, firs and spruce, as well as the spectacular *Magnolia grandiflora* from North America; oaks from America as well as the Mediterranean countries; and pines from Corsica and across the Atlantic. More mundanely, the new style reflected the changes in farming methods and hunting practice. Estates were being enclosed into fields as deer-hunting was replaced by fox-hunting, which called for the creation of small coverts in which foxes could breed. Hedges, ditches and rides cut through woodland now became the ideal setting for the hunt.

Finally, the new gardens were much more economical to maintain than their baroque predecessors, which had swallowed up fortunes in labour costs. Groves of trees, winding streams and cascades, temples and follies called for minimum upkeep compared with the clipping, pruning and pleaching of the parterres, *bosquets* and wildernesses of the previous century.

Bridgeman's and Caroline's modifications to Kensington showed the evolution of the new style. In Horace Walpole's assessment, 'though [Bridgeman] still adhered much to straight walks with high clipped hedges, they were only his great lines, the rest he diversified by wildernesses, and with loose groves of oak, though still within surrounding hedges'. The first sign that the old geometric style was coming to its end had been the introduction of winding walks at about the turn of the century. It was now the era of the wiggly walk. And this was to be the distinctive new feature of Kensington.

The first change was that the gardens ceased to be the Royal Paddock. The animals were despatched to the zoo in the Tower of London. Although George II would still hunt in the park, its chief role was to provide a place to walk and wander. For this, massive plantings of trees and shrubs were made. A vast grove of 12,103 elms, long since gone, was planted round the Round Pond followed by the making of 'serpentine walks' through plantings of evergreen and forest trees in the interstices of the formal avenues and by a 'walk of shade' encompassing the entire garden. Switzer listed the types of trees used for such plantings: field maple, hornbeam, common alder, beech, plane, poplar, wild cherry, oak, willow and elm.

The 'opening of the upper wilderness', it is recorded, was done '. . . as Her Majesty shall direct'. Whereas George I had attracted the odium of the populace by enclosing the gardens and keeping them for his own hunting use, Caroline threw them open to anyone deemed worthy of an admission ticket, obtained from the Lord Chamberlain. As a result Kensington Gardens became a fashionable resort for London society.

Even before the old King's death the bastions to the east of the string of ten oblong ponds formed by the river Westborne, a minor tributary of the Thames, had been constructed, with the resulting ravine acting as a ha-ha between the gardens and Hyde Park beyond. The invention of the ha-ha was important for the development of the new style, for it not only kept at bay the cattle and deer, which could not bound the ravine, but by dispensing with the need for enclosing walls, allowed the landscape beyond to form part of the garden experience. The bastions provided views over the new gardens as well as over Hyde Park and the earthworks which made them up are still visible, albeit shrubbed over. Their design, like the defence walls of a star-shaped fortress, recalled the bastions by Vanbrugh at Blenheim and Grimsthorpe, and must certainly have been part of his contribution to the scheme.

The ten oblong ponds which had been made for Queen Anne were joined together by Bridgeman to create the irregularly shaped lake we call the Serpentine. Work began on this in September 1730 and was completed by May of the following year. It forms a striking contrast with the formal treatment of water in the Round Pond. Soon all formal treatments of water would be abandoned but here the development was at an intermediary stage. It recalled the plan for a 'Rural and Extensive Garden' by Stephen Switzer, published in his *Ichnographia Rustica*, 1718, where a solitary irregular lake is distantly sited from the mansion house, with some twenty other formal treatments of water dotted around.

Bridgeman loved vast scale and, looking at the lake and the avenues and vistas to and from the palace today, one is still struck by how astonishingly grandiose his concept was. So huge are the gardens and so distracted are we now by the tarmacked paths criss-crossing seemingly everywhere, we can easily lose sight of what an amazing survival Kensington is. The avenues have of course been replanted three or four times since the 1720s, losing in places their original line, but great care is now being taken to reinstate the eighteenth-century scheme.

Although the Serpentine could have been Bridgeman's idea, it seems to show more the hand of William Kent. He certainly designed the Queen's Temple, with which the Serpentine is closely linked. Kent, like Bridgeman, came of humble stock. His talents were spotted by the local gentry, who paid for him to go to Italy, and thanks to those years and to his patronage by Lord Burlington, he became the innovative force associated with palladianism. In its simplest terms this was a rejection of the baroque in favour of a renewed study not only of classical antiquity but of the masters of its revival in the Renaissance: in Italy, Palladio, in England, Inigo Jones.

Bridgeman is likely to have known Kent as far back as 1719 and he must have watched his progress from painting to interior decoration to architecture and, by the 1720s, to garden design. Kent, it seems, could be brought in to alter or modify something initially laid out by Bridgeman but equally the two men could work together, as they did for Queen Caroline, which makes it difficult to establish where the work of one ended and that of the other began. If to Bridgeman we owe the gradual dissolution of the old symmetry in favour of the serpentine line, to Kent we owe the deployment of the garden as fundamentally a vehicle for the creation of pictures. The garden became theatre, a series of staged scenes through which the visitor walked. Its repertory consisted of statues, inscriptions, obelisks, columns, cascades and temples, which the visitor was called upon to read. These were arranged within a terrain of slopes and hillocks on which trees were massed in groups to achieve a chiaroscuro response to the fall of light. Such compositions evoked in three dimensions a classical arcady of a kind admired in the landscape paintings of Claude Lorraine.

Kent's contribution to Kensington Gardens was a tableau precisely of this kind. It was prefaced by his design for a revolving summerhouse to top a mount constructed from the earth excavated to make the Serpentine. The mount is still perceptible today, although now it is shrubbed over to conceal public lavatories. Originally, a winding path flanked by trees and shrubs led up to the summerhouse, which was built in 1733 and would have been an ideal vantage point from which the Queen could look either to the south towards St James's Palace and Park or west across her own gardens back to Kensington Palace.

Much more significant was the Temple, which was commissioned in October 1734, for here for the first time was picture-making in the Kent manner. Its site was one of the enclosures within the formal avenues to the west of the Serpentine. By cutting down the trees a vista was made that sloped away from the Temple directly to the water's edge, affording a delightful view for the occupants of the building. Probably even more delightful was the view from the opposite banks of the lake, a vista in which groups of trees framed a classical temple reflected in the calm waters of the Serpentine. This was the pastoral elysium of Virgil and Ovid materialized.

The King and Queen's public promenades in the new Kensington Gardens became an established part of court life. When Caroline had first come to England she and her husband had walked every day in St James's Park but soon she complained that it 'stank of people' and they migrated to Kensington. These daily walks developed into a kind of informal court which allowed access to the royal family to others besides those who attended the court drawing-rooms and levées. And they became the subject of popular satire in which the fast-walking George II, with his curious strutting step, forged ahead, leaving his ample consort puffing behind.

Kensington's glories were nevertheless but a preliminary foray for Caroline's greatest creation, Richmond Gardens, which survive today partly as a section of the Royal Botanic Gardens Kew

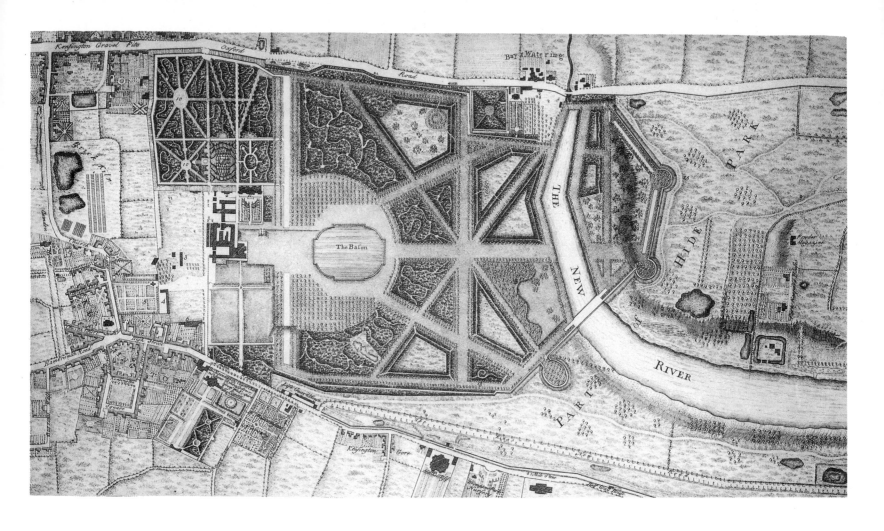

KENSINGTON GARDENS
as laid out between 1726 and 1734, survive remarkably intact. Their planning shows a dramatic evolution in garden style within only a few years from monumental formality to the new taste for serpentine curves. Today (*left*), the broad groundplan of three major avenues radiating out from a large semicircle which looked back to the previous century is still discernable, while the winding, irregular paths which belong to the eighteenth century have disappeared. The map by John Rocque of *c.* 1756 (*above*) shows that although the Stuart gardens to the south of the palace had vanished by then, the wilderness made for Queen Anne to the north of the palace was still intact.

THE MOUNT IN KENSINGTON
Gardens (*left*) was constructed
in 1733. The mount had been
a feature of sixteenth-century
gardens but was used here to
meet the new demand for
views that embraced the
landscape beyond the garden.
At the top was a classical
summerhouse with flanking
caryatids, known as a Windsor
seat. Because it revolved,
Caroline could look back to
the palace and, in the opposite
direction, down to Green Park,
St James's and Westminster. In
A. B. Lens's wash drawing of
1736 the mount is viewed
from what was known as the
King's New Road or the Route
de Roi, from which Rotten
Row derives its name, and
which was one of the first
highways to be illuminated as
a deterrent to footpads.

and the remainder as a golf course in Richmond Park, although sadly not a single feature of the Richmond Gardens Caroline created can be traced. The attraction of Richmond, which was purchased in 1719 by the Prince of Wales as a summer residence, lay not only in its proximity to London but in the hundred acres of grounds which included riverside walks. Caroline began work at least as early as 1726 on transforming all of this area into one of the most famous of early eighteenth-century gardens.

On his accession in 1727 George II gave Richmond Lodge to Caroline as her dower palace. Although there was already a garden, in which George London is likely to have had a hand, to all intents and purposes what she created was the work of Bridgeman and Kent. Rocque's map of 1748, eleven years after her death, shows her garden still intact and gives a powerful impression of its originality, for it boldly strikes out away from Richmond Lodge and colonizes an irregular array of fields scattered across the farmed landscape which it embraced.

In that lay its novelty. It was written at the time 'that all the varieties of nature are to be seen within those grounds, and all the improvements of art. Had Milton been living, his description of paradise . . . would, in great measure, have been thought to be drawn from the view of this palace.' Eden as described by Milton was one of the gospels of the new landscape art, and

Richmond is indeed a very different gardening world from Kensington. Its inspiration was also drawn from classical antiquity. Robert Castell's book, *The Villas of the Ancients Illustrated*, dedicated to William Kent's patron, Lord Burlington, had been published in 1728 and attempted to depict the gardens of such villas, basing the re-creation on classical texts and what was still to be seen in Italy.

Villa gardens were thought to be filled with temples and sculpture, and, even more important, the garden and the farmed landscape were seen to interpenetrate. This offered opportunities for endless variety and contrast in design: ascents and descents, symmetrical as against asymmetrical parts, different uses of water from winding streams to cascades, architecture both within and outside the confines of the garden. The aim was to give as many agreeable views as possible.

Bridgeman's work at Richmond was revolutionary in introducing cultivated fields, and even tiny pockets of seeming forest, within the garden vista. Old-fashioned straight lines were still included, as the groundplan reveals, but symmetry had virtually gone. Kent's role was complementary to but different from Bridgeman's, for he gave visual substance to the Queen's ideals by composing 'pictures' which would engage visitors in an awareness of Caroline's intellectual and philosophical inclinations, above all those which demonstrated her patriotism and

THE QUEEN'S TEMPLE
in Kensington Gardens was
designed by William Kent and
built in 1734. A small,
rusticated classical building, it
marked a revolution in royal
garden-making: by cutting a
swath through the formal
avenue of trees to the west of
the Serpentine, Caroline was
given an uninterrupted vista
that sloped to the water's edge,
while from the opposite bank
the Temple could be seen
across the reflective waters in
its setting of trees.

THE ORIGINAL PICTORIAL EFFECT
of an arcadian tableau inspired
by classical antiquity is
captured (*left*) in a detail from
an engraving by John Tinney
of 1744. The Temple still
stands (*above*) and has recently
been restored, although sadly
not its immediate setting, so
that it can no longer be viewed
from the other side of the
Serpentine.

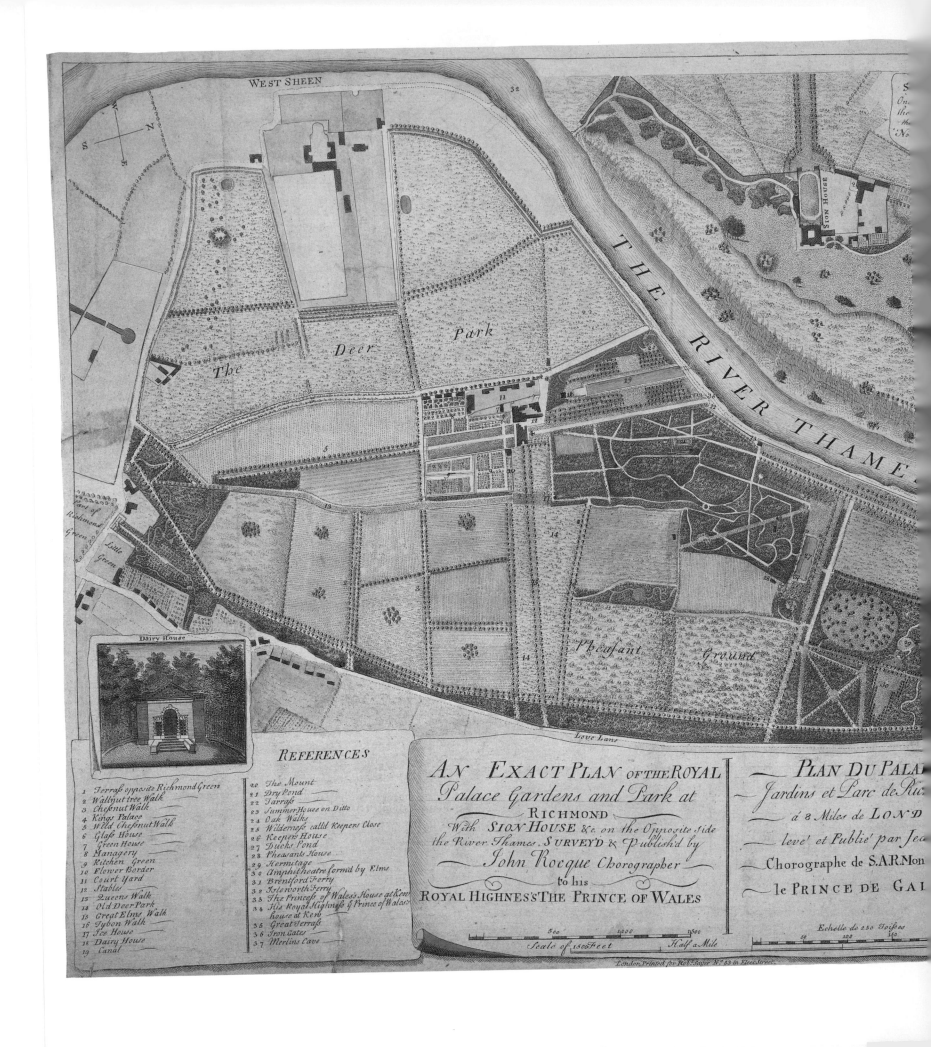

WEST SHEEN

32

SION HOUSE

THE RIVER THAMES

The Deer Park

Dairy House

Pheasant Ground

Love Lane

REFERENCES

1 Terrass opposite Richmond Green
2 Walnut tree Walk
3 Chesnut Walk
4 Kings Palace
5 Wild Chesnut Walk
6 Glass House
7 Green House
8 Managery
9 Kitchen Green
10 Flower Border
11 Court Yard
12 Stables
13 Queens Walk
14 Old Deer Park
15 Great Elms Walk
16 Tybon Walk
17 Ice House
18 Dairy House
19 Canal

20 The Mount
21 Dry Pond
22 Tarrass
23 Summer House on Ditto
24 Oak Walks
25 Wilderness call'd Keepers Close
26 Keepers House
27 Ducks Pond
28 Pheasants House
29 Hermitage
30 Amphitheatre form'd by Elms
31 Brentford Ferry
32 Ixtenworth Ferry
33 The Princess of Wales's House at Kew
34 His Royal Highness ye Prince of Wales's house at Kew
35 Great Terrass
36 Iron Gates
37 Merlins Cave

AN EXACT PLAN OF THE ROYAL
Palace Gardens and Park at
RICHMOND
With SION HOUSE &c. on the Opposite Side
the River Thames. SURVEY'D & Publish'd by
John Rocque Chorographer
to his
ROYAL HIGHNESS'S THE PRINCE OF WALES

PLAN DU PALAI
Jardins et Parc de Ric
á 8 Miles de LOND
levé et Publié par Jea
Chorographe de S.A.R. Mon
le PRINCE DE GA

500   1000   1500
Scale of 1500 Feet   Half a Mile

Echelle de 250 Toises
50   100   150

London, Printed for Rob.t Sayer N.o 53 in Fleet Street.

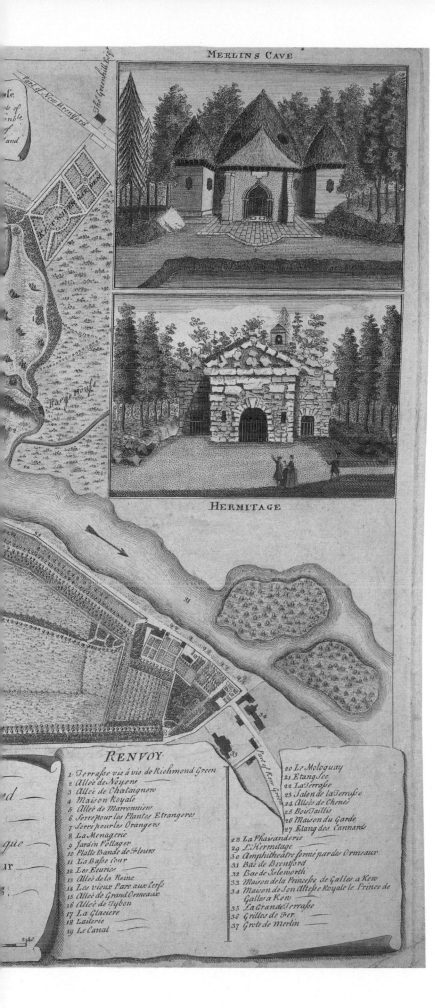

MERLIN'S CAVE

HERMITAGE

RENVOY

1. Terrasse vis à vis de Richmond Green
2. Allée de Noyers
3. Allée de Chataigners
4. Maison Royale
5. Allée de Marronniers
6. Serre pour les Plantes Etrangeres
7. Serre pour les Orangers
8. La Menagerie
9. Jardin Potager
10. Platte Bande de Fleurs
11. La Basse Cour
12. Les Ecuries
13. Allée de la Reine
14. Les vieux Parc aux Cerfs
15. Allée de Grand Ormeaux
16. Allée de Tybon
17. La Glaciere
18. Laiterie
19. Le Canal

20. Le Moloquay
21. Etang See
22. La Terrasse
23. Salon de la Terrasse
24. Allée de Chenes
25. Bois Taillis
26. Maison du Garde
27. Etang des Cannards
28. La Phaisanderie
29. L'Hermitage
30. Amphitheatre formé par des Ormeaux
31. Bac de Brentford
32. Bac de Isleworth
33. Maison de la Princesse de Galles a Kew
34. Maison de Son Altesse Royale le Prince de Galles a Kew
35. La Grande Terrasse
36. Grilles de Fer
37. Grote de Merlin

JOHN ROCQUE'S MAP OF 1748 RECORDS QUEEN CAROLINE'S GARDEN at Richmond, which was laid out in 1726. Visitors toured the hundred-acre garden by a carefully thought out set route. This began at Richmond Lodge (4) with the Dairy (18) at the head of a canal (19) which stretched down to the Thames, where there was a temple (20) on a small mount. Having enjoyed the views there, visitors returned to the Dairy, then crossed over the long formal gravel path which led to the river and went into the wood in which there was the Queen's Pavilion. The route then led back to the river and a banqueting house (23), and from there, via a wilderness (25) to Merlin's Cave (37) and on by way of the Forest Oval to the Hermitage (29). After this, visitors went on to see the amphitheatre (30) and then followed the outer perimeter of the gardens along Love Lane, looking across fields, and left the gardens by going through a small wilderness, exiting at Richmond Green (1).

RICHMOND'S TWO MOST FAMOUS GARDEN BUILDINGS, BOTH BY William Kent, the Hermitage and Merlin's Cave, are inset into the Rocque map at the top right. The Hermitage, erected in 1732, was a ruin without but within had an elegant palladian interior that included marble busts of philosophers and scientists, reflecting Caroline's intellectual interests. Merlin's Cave, a thatched gothick cottage built in 1735, was an eccentric garden building whose roof even sprouted fir trees. It is seen (above) in a cross-section by J. Vardy of c.1744. Inside it consisted of a circular room, with openings on three sides, which housed a library for the use of the thresher-poet, Stephen Duck, who was its caretaker. Its most surprising feature was a waxwork tableau which centred on the figure of Merlin prophesying not only the accession of the House of Tudor to the British throne but also that of Hanover. The political message of Merlin's Cave was the subject of sustained ridicule by those opposed to the policies of prime minister Sir Robert Walpole, who was closely allied to Queen Caroline.

Today Richmond Gardens have totally disappeared, one of the few royal gardens laid out after 1600 to be completely lost. The house was demolished and part of the garden has been subsumed into those of the present day Royal Botanic Gardens at Kew, and part into a golf course.

THE IMPERIAL THEME

PRINCESS AUGUSTA, MOTHER OF GEORGE III

Augusta of Saxe-Gotha (1719–72), Princess of Wales, is a little known figure. But it is largely to her that we owe the Royal Botanic Gardens at Kew today and a royal commitment to the study of botany that was to be of crucial importance in placing Britain at the forefront of every new development in botanical science by the close of the eighteenth century. Her personal initiative would probably not, however, have been possible without her having first been made aware of the garden revolution taking place in England by her husband, Frederick, Prince of Wales (1707–51).

The youngest daughter of the ruler of a small Protestant North German state, Augusta had been brought up by her mother in the country in virtual seclusion until, in 1735, she was taken to the court of Prussia to be viewed by George II as the possible wife for his hated son and heir, Frederick. She must have passed muster, although she spoke no English and little French; her mother believed that after twenty years of Hanoverian rule the British spoke German. Frederick, still smarting from the slight of the King marrying off his sister, the Princess Royal, before him, made no objection,

PRINCESS AUGUSTA; A DETAIL OF A PORTRAIT OF AN UNKNOWN DATE
from the studio of Allan Ramsay. During the years of her widowhood,
particularly between 1757 and 1763, the creation of the gardens at
Kew became her passion.

THE MOST FAMOUS GARDEN BUILDING IN THE COUNTRY AT THE TIME IT WAS
built in 1762, the Pagoda at Kew was one of almost thirty structures
dotted through Princess Augusta's hundred-acre garden. Although still
striking in appearance, it was originally far more exotic: its roofs
glittered with glazed tiles and were adorned with eighty brilliantly
coloured dragons. It was not conceived as an exact replica of a
Chinese pagoda but as a fantasy to evoke a civilization just beginning
to be studied and admired.

particularly since marriage would mean an increase in his annual allowance.

The wedding took place before the assembled court in April 1736, when the seventeen-year-old princess was described by the acerbic Lord Hervey as 'rather tall, and had health and youth enough in her face joined to a very modest and good-natured look, to make her countenance not disagreeable'. She was, however, 'very ill-made, a good deal awry, her arms long, and her motions awkward' and, to add a final blow, 'in spite of all the finery of jewels and brocade, [has] an ordinary air which no trappings could cover or exalt'.

Lord Hervey, Queen Caroline's confidant, was unlikely to take a sympathetic view of Augusta, for the Queen no less than the King loathed Frederick and long before the marriage the violent fissure between father and son, which echoed that in the previous generation, had resulted in the emergence of a separate court around the Prince of Wales, attracting to it those who formed the Opposition to the ruling Whig government of Sir Robert Walpole. There is no biography of Augusta but her portraits show that, although her features cannot be described as other than a trifle bovine, they and her eyes are not devoid of intelligence or humour, both attributes essential to survival in royal family life in the middle of the eighteenth century and particularly so if married to Frederick.

Born in 1707, the Prince was seven when his father came to the throne and he was kept in Hanover out of harm's way until he came of age at twenty-one. Short of stature, with a chubby pink face and pale aquamarine eyes, Frederick had a character that left much to be desired. He was wayward, devious and over-excitable, with a passion for women. But he also had his good side, being 'conversable and void of ceremony', and, unlike both his father and grandfather, he loved the arts and was to be the most discerning royal patron and collector between Charles I and George IV. He genuinely enjoyed the society of artists and appointed as his Principal Painter the Frenchman, Philippe Mercier, who broke the mould of existing royal portraiture by investing it with a new sinuous elegance and liveliness, a style we now define as rococo. In his gardening schemes, too, Frederick was prepared to break new ground.

In 1732, four years before his marriage to Augusta, he had purchased Carlton House, London, which occupied the space roughly taken today by the Athenaeum Club on Pall Mall, at the head of Duke of York's Steps. It was acquired from the major patron of the arts, Lord Burlington, who may have proposed to the Prince that he use his protégé, William Kent, to re-lay out the garden. The twelve-acre garden ran along the south front of Carlton House, looking over the Mall into St James's Park. Part of it covered the site of the old Privy Garden of St James's Palace where only a few years before had stood what survived of André Mollet's garden for Charles II. Kent built a domed palladian temple reminiscent of Burlington's villa at Chiswick at right angles to the house, from which there was a vista, flanked by exedras of trellis-work, down towards a cascade and pool surrounded by irregular groves of young trees. Nothing of the garden survives but an engraving of 1760 shows the view looking back to Kent's temple. The composition, although loose, is still basically symmetrical. Frederick's garden, like his mother's, was political. On the steps of the temple stood busts of Edward III's son, the Black Prince, and the Saxon King Alfred by Rysbrack. The former embodied a heroic ideal as a Prince of Wales, the latter was the founder of British liberties and the constitution.

Horace Walpole stated categorically that the Carlton House garden was 'borrowed from the poet's at Twickenham', the poet being Alexander Pope, whose famous garden at Twickenham had been made in the 1720s and was a pioneer shrine of the new style. Pope's garden too was small and had a central vista runing to a focal point which was an obelisk in memory of his mother, flanked on either side by groves of trees. Straight and serpentine walks ran through the groves and the entire composition was punctuated with urns and sculpture intended to stir the imagination. 'All gardening is landscape painting,' Pope declared in 1734, the year Kent, who knew Pope's garden well, finished Carlton House. Kent's painterly vista only differed significantly from Pope's in that it did not run straight from the house but had to be formed from a cross-axis running east to west across the garden façade.

The garden was completed in two years and its impact can be gauged from a letter of 23 December 1734 from Sir Thomas Robinson, a much-travelled amateur architect, to his father-in-law, the Earl of Carlisle; he described it as 'more diversified and of greater variety than anything . . . I ever saw' and he went on to say how it had 'the appearance of beautiful nature' and to give a new source for the style, China, for its design was 'entirely after their models where they never plant straight lines or make regular designs'.

Robinson is certainly wrong in billing the garden at Carlton House as a fount for a 'new style in gardening', for the break with the geometric style was already well advanced in 1730. All the same it must have been a striking instance of the new irregular manner, and all the more eye-catching because it was not a revision or addition, like Kent's work for Frederick's mother at Kensington and Richmond, but a completely new, if comparatively small, garden.

When Frederick had acquired Kew in 1729 as his summer residence, it must have been an additional irritant to his parents, for the estate, centred on what was called the White House, which no longer exists, was contiguous to his mother's at Richmond. Eventually the two were to be made one but in the eighteenth century they were divided by the inappropriately named Love Lane. The present Botanic Gardens cover an area which is an amalgam of a small part of Caroline's vast Richmond Gardens and most of the much smaller acreage which made up Frederick's Kew. Under its previous owners, the Capell

THE MAIN VISTA OF FREDERICK, Prince of Wales's innovative garden at Carlton House leads the eye towards a classical temple backed by groves of young trees. Woollet's engraving of *c.*1760 (*above*) also shows mirror-image semicircles of trellis-work looking into pools of water and the foregrounds of the shrubberies crammed with flowers. Laid out between 1732 and 1734, it was intended to evoke an idealized vision of the classical world but with contemporary political overtones – on the steps leading up to the temple stood busts of the Black Prince and King Alfred, both heroes of the party then in Opposition.

CLASSICAL TERMS, BUSTS OF figures which merged into tapering pedestals, by the sculptor Peter Scheemakers were among the fine sculpture commissioned for the gardens at Carlton House. They were placed in facing pairs to accentuate the perspective to the temple (*above*). Today they are inappropriately sited in the re-created formal garden (*left*) behind the Dutch House at Kew Gardens.

FREDERICK, PRINCE OF WALES'S NEW GARDEN AT KEW
surrounded the White House, and is seen here (*left*) in a painting by
J.J. Schalk of *c*.1759. (The White House stood near the present Dutch
House but was demolished in 1802 to make way for a sumptuous
new palace for George III that was, in the end, never built). Frederick
acquired the house in 1729 and had it remodelled as a palladian villa.
But it was not until about twenty years later, and only three years
before he died, that he began to create a major new garden in the
adjacent land. Work came to a halt on the Prince's death in 1751 but
by then the distinctive character and style of the garden had already
been established. It was striking for its tree-scape: we know that his
planting included 'many curious & forain Trees exotics', a horticultural
commitment that was quite new and set Kew apart from other royal
gardens. It was to have been a garden with serpentine paths
punctuated by encounters with extraordinary garden buildings and
sculptural tableaux designed to evoke both other ages and other
civilizations. The only one known to have been completed was the
House of Confucius, which can be seen nestling in the greenery to the
right. Later re-sited and incorporated into the second phase of the
garden's development under Frederick's widow, Princess Augusta, it
was one of the most famous of Kew's garden buildings. Chinoiserie
was the height of garden fashion during the 1730s and 1740s and the
wooden garden pavilion, sketched by G. E. Papendiek in the early
nineteenth century (*above*), would have been brilliantly painted and
gilded. Inside it was decorated with scenes connected with the life and
work of the Chinese philosopher, Confucius. In this way it combined
use as a summerhouse with matter for thought about a non-European
philosophy of life which, at that period, was becoming a subject of
great fascination.

family, Kew had already acquired a horticultural reputation, particularly for its fine trees and shrubs which included variegated hollies, standard laurustinus and orange trees which were protected by a hedge of silver firs.

The Prince had commissioned Kent to refurbish the house, which was virtually rebuilt, and it was probably Kent who was responsible for the initial landscaping of his garden: the house looked on to a smooth lawn flanked by trees in the new pictorial manner. Serious work did not, however, begin on the gardens at Kew until 1749, the year after Kent died, thirteen years after Frederick's marriage to Augusta and shortly after the arrival on the scene of John Stuart, 3rd Earl of Bute, who was to be a key figure in the creation of Kew.

Bute was an impoverished Scottish nobleman who had recouped his fortunes by a spectacular marriage to the heiress, Mary Wortley Montagu. His knowledge of botany and what was to be a lifelong interest in gardening was already established when he came south in 1745 at the age of thirty. He was a strikingly handsome man with legs which were regarded as the most elegant in London. With his passionate love for the arts and for theatre and masquerade, as well as his political ambitions, he seemed destined for the rival court. When he met the Prince of Wales in 1747 he was immediately taken up and became close to both Frederick and Augusta, and in October 1750 he was made a Lord of the Bedchamber. It was at this period that he was instrumental to the Prince's works at Kew, which went on simultaneously with those on his own estate at Kenwood House on Hampstead Heath, London, which, he wrote in 1751, he was 'filling with every exotic our climate will protect'.

The extent of Bute's involvement in Kew is apparent in a letter written by Thomas Knowlton on 13 November 1758, which tells of the construction of a 300-foot-long heated greenhouse for tender plants which Bute was collecting from agents established all over the world: 'for to be sure, my lord is the most knowing of any in the kingdom. . . and he is the person as has prompted the young prince'. From the onset Kew was as much to do with plants as it was with buildings and other aspects of design, and therefore very different from any of its predecessors. By 1749 both the Royal Gardeners, Bridgeman and Kent, were dead and 'Capability' Brown was not to leave Stowe until the year of the Prince's death. The indications are that Bute was its designer, acting as amanuensis to the Prince, an arrangement which was to be reactivated with his widow.

A CARTOUCHE OF PRINCESS AUGUSTA'S MONOGRAM
added by William IV to her Orangery at Kew.

By Frederick's death in 1751 the elements which were to make Kew so distinctive were already in place. It was to be a horticultural and botanical experience, a tour through strange and exotic trees and plants growing both in the open and in the greenhouse. Caroline's Richmond had none of this and, although the rigid geometrical lay-out had begun to be broken there, here at Kew it must have completely gone, with winding and meandering paths that meant that each new scene came as a surprise. It is a garden style categorized as rococo. As visitors progressed through the serpentine and undulating walkways of such a terrain they would have encountered not only monuments evocative of the classical world, as at Richmond or Kensington, but also ones designed to conjure up the civilizations of the East: India, Islam and China.

By the mid-1740s the vogue for chinoiserie was at its height and 1747 saw the publication in English of Père Attiret's highly influential descriptions of Chinese imperial gardens. European knowledge of the reality of Chinese gardens was flimsy but one fact universally believed about them was that they were irregular. Sir William Temple in his *The Gardens of Epicurus* (1685) had first coined the Chinese word 'sharawadgi' to describe that irregularity. Not only did the idea catch on and contribute to the break up of the geometric gardens but also by the 1730s led to the proliferation of Chinese-style garden ornamen-tation. Richard or 'Dickie' Bateman pioneered the 'Sharawadgi taste' in England and his famous garden at Old Windsor, which was certainly complete by 1741, was a likely influence on the making of Kew during its first phase under Frederick.

George Vertue, chronicler of the arts in early Georgian England, describes going to see the 'new Chinesia summer house painted in their style and ornaments the story of Confucius and his doctrines'. This was the famous House of Confucius with its pagoda roof, dragon finials, tingling bells and fretwork. Although it was possibly the work of the architect Sir William Chambers, it is generally regarded as having been designed by Joseph Goupy, who certainly painted the interior.

This representative of the Orient at Kew was to be complemented by symbols of the philosophical traditions of the West and Vertue was asked by the Prince for engravings of ancient and modern philosophers from which a set of busts could be made to adorn an artificial Mount Parnassus. The mount, a feature typical of the villa gardens of Renaissance Italy asserting that the place was a home of the Muses and civilization, was to be constructed from the earth excavated for an aquaduct across the grounds. Frederick also had purchased for him in Italy thirteen life-sized marble statues by the late sixteenth-century sculptor, Pietro Francavilla. The Prince was to die before these superb pieces were shipped and they were still languishing unopened in their cases in a shed at Kew in 1786. After a tortuous history only seven of these statues appear to have survived: four once stood in the East Terrace Garden at Windsor Castle but are now in the Orangery in Kensington Gardens, two are on loan from the present Kew Gardens to the Victoria & Albert Museum and one is in the Wadsworth Athenaeum, Hartford, Connecticut.

The Prince of Wales died in March 1751, before his garden scheme could be fully realized. He was killed by gardening, according to George Vertue, who described how Frederick had contracted a fatal chill after being caught in a rainstorm while out directing the works at Kew. It was the widowed Augusta who would now transform the garden.

For most of her married life Augusta remains a shadowy figure, totally dominated by her husband, acquiescent in his long succession of amours, and only too anxious to appease feuding parties. But, like her mother-in-law, she was privy to all his political manoeuvrings and this involvement later resulted in a determination not to allow her eldest son's bride any political power. Augusta produced no less than nine children and also seems almost to have been educated by Frederick. For example, she took drawing lessons from one of his favourite artists, Joseph Goupy. And through her husband she came under the influence of Bute, with whom she formed a close liaison.

Augusta was only thirty-two when Frederick died and her twelve-year-old son George, the new Prince of Wales, became destined to succeed the elderly George II. She now assumed a dominant role as mother of the future monarch, rarely letting him out of her sight and admonishing him to be autocratic: 'George, be King.' He succeeded on the death of his grandfather in 1760 and though Augusta's dominance over him gradually ceased after his marriage in 1761, she was seen to be behind George III's reassertion of the royal prerogative and his favouring of Bute, who became prime minister in 1762. Even before she was widowed, the alliance of Augusta and Bute, which seemed to end with his abandonment of politics in 1763, had been the subject of the malicious pen of Horace Walpole.

Five years after Frederick's death Augusta and Bute together embarked on the most stupendous royal garden extravaganza of the century. All of this was accomplished at huge cost in the short period between 1757 and 1763, against a political background of considerable importance, for Augusta, like her husband and mother-in-law, used the royal garden as a vehicle for political statements and a celebration of ideals. It was no coincidence that the garden schemes at Kew were reactivated the year after the Prince of Wales was given a substantial allowance by his grandfather in the hope that he would set up his own household. The Prince, however, continued to live a cloistered life with his mother and appointed Bute as his chief instructor and groom of the stole. Meanwhile the war which had broken out against France and Austria in 1756 had progressed from

disaster to triumph, with naval and military victories around the globe; the defeat of the French in Canada by Wolfe and in India by Clive were in effect to create the British Empire. It was amid this atmosphere of imperial triumph that George ascended the throne in 1760 and brought to an end the long Whig dominance in favour of the Tories and Bute, although Bute would prove so unpopular that he would resign in April 1763, two months after the Treaty of Paris which closed the war.

This was the backcloth to the creation of Kew Gardens, whose splendours were publicized to the whole of Europe in 1763 in a sumptuous commemorative volume by William Chambers, *Plans, Elevations, Sections, and Perspective Views of the Gardens and Buildings at Kew*, the cost of which was met not by Augusta but the new King. Every aspect of this publication was closely supervised by Sir William Chambers, who had been appointed on Bute's recommendation as architectural tutor to the Prince and architect to Augusta in 1756. Born of Scottish parents in Sweden, Chambers had in his youth visited China where he sketched buildings and studied Chinese culture; his *Designs for Chinese Buildings*, published in 1756, gained him an undeserved reputation as a sinologist.

Although Chambers is credited with the designs for the layout of the new gardens at Kew, his role was probably that of amanuensis to Bute and Augusta, and Chambers himself made Augusta's passionate input clear: 'The prince employs me three mornings in a week to teach him architecture . . . The princess has the rest of the week, which is scarcely sufficient as she is for ever adding new embellishments at Kew, [in] all [of] which I direct the execution [and] measure the work.'

The gardens at Kew covered a long awkward tongue of land and the view was turned inwards, to the contemplation at the centre of a large irregularly shaped lake with an island, reached by a bridge (built in a night), and two fields. These were farmed and access to them was by a viaduct disguised as a ruined classical arch which still survives. Deep ha-has made a clear visual distinction between unadorned nature, in the form of cows and sheep grazing, and the frame in which they had been set, where nature had been tamed by the power of art.

This interplay of garden and agriculture looks back to what had been such an original feature in Caroline's Richmond Gardens, and indeed the meandering walkway, punctuated by almost thirty garden buildings that encompassed the garden, was in spirit still rococo. Kew was in fact a rococo garden in neoclassical garb with little that was frivolous about it.

The buildings included seven highly sophisticated classical temples by Chambers, all of them richly ornamented. Three, dedicated to Arethusa, Aeolus and Bellona, are still there, although the latter two have been re-sited. The Temple of the Sun, which was of lath and plaster and only collapsed in 1916, was an imitation of that amidst the Roman ruins at Baalbeck in the Lebanon, which had only been recently discovered and excavated by Chambers' friend, Robert Wood, whose *The Ruins*

THE TEMPLE OF BELLONA AT KEW (*left*) is one of the few buildings which survive from 1760, although re-sited and today given a carpet of modern crocuses. Between 1757 and 1763, with the aid of the Earl of Bute and the architect – garden designer Sir William Chambers, Princess Augusta created a spectacular and unusual landscape on a narrow tongue of land. In an ambitious and far-reaching plan, fields and a lake at the centre of the garden were surrounded by a meandering walkway, planted as an arboretum with rare and exotic trees from around the globe, both evergreen and deciduous and elaborately underplanted with flowering shrubs and climbers. This provided the framework for the thirty or so celebratory and symbolic buildings constructed at vast cost and designed to call to mind eras and civilizations as varied as classical antiquity, the Middle Ages, China and Islam. Many of Chambers' buildings were of wood or only of lathe and plaster and therefore perishable; even by the late 1760s they required considerable annual maintenance by a host of carpenters, bricklayers, plumbers and painters. Bellona was the Roman goddess of war, an allusion both to the war being fought at that time against France and Austria, and to the ideals of the civilization upon which the eighteenth century still modelled itself.

THE LARGEST GARDEN BUILDING designed by Sir William Chambers for Princess Augusta at Kew was what is now known as the Orangery (*left*). The function of the greenhouse had changed and in the eighteenth century the serious glasshouse with its elaborate heating system, known at Kew as the Great Stove, housed the sub-tropical fruit and flowers; thus the Orangery, built in 1761, was released to take on a more decorative and social role as a garden building in which it became customary to drink tea, play at cards or read on a summer's evening amidst collections of fragrant, container-grown plants such as oleanders, myrtles and orange trees.

OVERLEAF: THE TEMPLE OF AEOLUS at Kew, dedicated to the Roman god of the winds, was built for Augusta between 1760 and 1763. Originally it contained a revolving seat from which it was possible to obtain different views of the gardens. Largely rebuilt and re-sited on this artificial hillock in 1845, it is now surrounded by a late Victorian naturalistic planting of bulbs and wild flowers.

of Balbec of 1757 was influential on the rapidly evolving neo-classical style. Most of the classical temples, however, were built in commemoration of the recent British military victories.

Through exploration and influence, as well as military victory, British hegemony was extending even further across the globe and this is reflected in the more extraordinary of the garden buildings, the Alhambra and the Pagoda, of which only the latter survives. They represented, as similar buildings had earlier, philosophies and ways of life fascinating to the Western mind, but by the 1760s they were also an aspect of British triumphalism. They were sited at the furthest point from the palace in the so-called wilderness and were perhaps given a planting indicative of their country of origin. The Pagoda was 160 feet high and at the time was the most ambitious chinoiserie garden structure in Europe. Its interior staircase is still intact but the exterior is a shadow of its former glory, when its roofs were covered with glazed tiles and supported some eighty huge and garishly coloured dragons. In its day it was a skyscraper. 'We begin to perceive the tower of Kew from Montpellier Row,' Horace Walpole wrote to Lord Strafford on 5 July 1761, 'in a fortnight you will see it from Yorkshire.'

This second group of buildings also included both a mosque, with an inscription in Arabic from the Koran, and a gothick cathedral – neither of which survives. The cathedral was designed by the Swiss artist earlier favoured by Frederick, Johann Heinrich Müntz, who was a major pioneer of gothick revival architecture. His cathedral at Kew was one of the most sumptuous and delicately ornamented gothick garden buildings of the century and was to have a considerable influence.

While Frederick's House of Confucius celebrating an Eastern philosopher may have been built to complement a Mount Parnassus, a symbolic representation of the Western philosophical

THE RUINED ARCH AT KEW, DESIGNED AS A RUIN BY SIR WILLIAM CHAMBERS,
acted as a viaduct, enabling the cattle and herdsmen to gain access to
the decorative yet productive fields at the centre of the garden, over
the path that wound round its perimeter. Sham ruins have a history
going back to the Renaissance but gained particular currency in
eighteenth-century England, calling on the visitor to muse upon the
transitory nature of even the greatest of past civilizations. The arch
would have also been viewed as a light-hearted caprice mocking time,
art and antiquity. Part of that element of play is caught in Richard
Wilson's painting of 1761–62 (*above*) when the arch was just two
years old. He took this double play further by deliberately depicting
the new building as though it were an ancient ruin in the Roman
Campagna. So successful was he that the picture passed as one of part
of the grounds of the Villa Borghese until 1949. It also makes an
eloquent plea for a proper restoration of what remains of the
arch today (*right*).

tradition, in Augusta's revision of Kew this theme was extended to include Islam and Christianity. For the first time serious consideration was being given to the religions of the Orient and, in contrast to the previous century's narrow-mindedness of dogma, there was now a striving towards an all-comprehensive, universal awareness of God. Augusta thus developed a topic which her mother-in-law in her generation had first explored within a solely Christian context in the Hermitage at Richmond. Kew can be seen as a true garden of the Enlightenment because it incorporated both artefacts and natural phenomena which provoked thoughts on the relationship of man and his creator.

Much of that was brought to mind through what, by the 1760s, was an old-fashioned means, symbolic buildings. By that date landscape design had moved on under the impetus of 'Capability' Brown, who was at his apogee during the years of the creation of Kew. In stark contrast, his gardens were virtually devoid of buildings and decoration. They were landscapes composed solely of undulating terrain, clumps of trees and shrubs, and sheets of water designed for man's free intelligence to roam as it were in Eden and regain a lost innocence. Thoughts on man's place in the scheme of things were prompted by compositions of these natural attributes alone, with use no longer made of a repertory of symbolism that had its roots in the Renaissance. Augusta's garden was rooted firmly in her husband's era and before, when the visitor had to make a tour by a set route, taking the mind through a succession of wide-ranging thoughts and attitudes by means of a series of pictorial tableaux.

Although the garden's main source of amazement at the time was its quantity of buildings, its botanical aspect also set it apart and, in the long run, was to dominate the history of Kew. During the creation of the garden, Bute's uncle, the arboriculturalist, Archibald Campbell, 3rd Duke of Argyll, died. At Whitton, near Hounslow in Middlesex, he had assembled one of the most famous of all collections of trees, besides maintaining a heated greenhouse crammed with rarities, and on his death the pick of these passed to Augusta at Kew, including a cedar of Lebanon (which fell on the Temple of the Sun), Turkey oak, *Ginkgo biloba*, persimmon and Hermes oak. They were followed by a further selection on the sale of Whitton in 1765. Throughout the 1760s baskets of 'new' plants and parcels of seeds continued to be sent to the Princess for her garden at Kew from other plantsmen in Britain, Europe and further afield. The importance of these new species in changing the garden's appearance can hardly be underestimated for they immeasurably enlarged the palette of the designer. 'The introduction of foreign trees and plants,' wrote Horace Walpole, dipping his pen into perspicacity instead of venom for a change, 'contributed essentially to the richness of colouring. . . . The mixture of various greens, the contrast between our forest then and the northern and West Indian firs and pines, are improvements.' A few trees from Augusta's time, such as the *Ginkgo biloba* and a *Sophora japonica*, still stand at Kew.

Bute was also instrumental in the appointment of two other key members of the Kew team, Sir John Hill and William Aiton, under whose custodianship Kew's botanical reputation grew ever more famous. Hill was employed in 1760, on George III's accession, as gardener at Kensington but spending a few days each week at Kew. Here he was responsible for superintending the laying out and subsequent maintenance of the nine acres set aside for Augusta's Physic or Botanic Garden, the ancestor of the Royal Botanic Gardens of today. Botanic gardens combined the study and codification of God's creation in the world of plants, gathered into one space, with the spirit of scientific inquiry into the natural world typical of the Enlightenment. In his *An idea of a botanic garden, in England: with lectures on the science*, published in 1758, Hill had first proposed the establishment of a royal botanic garden at Kensington, with lectures held on Saturdays while the court was at Richmond. Botanic gardens under royal auspices were monarchical status symbols, and a symbol that the British crown lacked. Louis XV was passionately interested in the scientific study of plants and by 1758 had established a major botanic garden at the Petit Trianon. And there was a similar garden at the imperial palace at Schönbrunn in Vienna.

To help establish Augusta's Botanic Garden, William Aiton was engaged in 1759. Also a Scot, Aiton had worked as an assistant to the celebrated Philip Miller at the Chelsea Physic Garden and he was to remain at Kew until his death in 1793. Although Hill, a prolific author, would publish the first catalogue of plants grown at Kew in 1768, Aiton, with considerable help from Banks's assistants, Solander and Dryander, later wrote a major work, *Hortus Kewensis* (1789), which listed some 5600 of the plants then growing at Kew, noting when they had been introduced to the country, and he became one of the most celebrated gardeners of his day.

The Physic Garden, destined to become the 'amplest and best collection of curious plants in Europe', contained the famous Great Stove as well as many smaller hot-houses that ensured the survival of rare plants from warmer climes, particularly from Australia and South Africa. A Scottish botanist visiting Kew in 1766 gives a rare glimpse of the practicalities. His account is full of notes such as: 'soil acid sandy, Mr Aiton puts rotten dung upon it every 2nd year; trees in the lawn protected from sheep by stakes placed in an inverted cone – almost all the borders covered with black earth – not one pile of grass in the garden – the bed covers slope from the south – moveable baskets, shrubs supported in every branch'. Plant name after plant name is followed by an exclamation mark of astonishment. The large list includes, for example, '*Erica triflora*, 12 feet, it perfumes the whole place', '*Clematis crispa, Phlox anemone [Anemone pavonina], Carthamus lanatus, Glycine [Wisteria] frutescens* – beautiful, all very beautiful'. The contents of the greenhouse leave him in a frenzy: '*Asclepias curaslavica*!', '*Phytolacca icosandria*! it stains', 'Caperbush [*Capparis spinosa*] on trellis 10 feet high coming in to fruit'. The

THE AVIARY AND FLOWER GARDEN AT KEW, PICTURED IN A WATERCOLOUR OF *c.*1763 by William Marlow (*above*), stood in a small but complex section of the gardens that also included the menagerie, the hot-houses and the Physic or Botanic Gardens. In spite of the triumph of the landscape style which relegated flower gardens to a separate enclosure, usually screened by trees and shrubs, there was still a passionate interest in flowers in the eighteenth century, especially in the new varieties pouring in from South Africa, Australia and the Americas. Flowers were still treated like botanical specimens, rather than used as part of a pictorial composition in terms of its shape and colour.

THE WILDERNESS AT KEW, A WATERCOLOUR OF *c.*1763 BY THOMAS SANDBY (*opposite*) captures better than almost anything else the actual experience of visiting Augusta's Kew. A lady and two men can be seen pausing to admire the Pagoda on their peregrination from one garden building to the next, each of which was set within a lavish planting of rare trees and shrubs. A tour involved encircling the agricultural heart of the garden; the ravine and fence to the right enclosed the central fields and ensured that the cattle did not stray. The visitors are in the most exotic part of the garden. To reach the Pagoda, they would have just passed the Moorish Alhambra and will arrive next at the Islamic Mosque.

hot-houses and their construction are considered in detail: 'No 1 without flue for African plants'; '2 w[i]th flue – Cape plants, ficordes and Gerania', and '3 for Indian plants'.

The Physic or Exotic Garden was never part of the main pleasure grounds but one section of a highly complex area, located close to the White House (in the north-east part of the gardens today). The area included the Flower Garden, reached through a splendid decorated archway, with a large aviary to one side and, not far from it, the menagerie or pheasant ground. Pens here contained Chinese and Tartarean pheasants, and other exotic birds, with goldfish swimming in the surrounding waters. This whole complex is of crucial importance not only in the story of the emergence of the Botanic Gardens at Kew but also in the revival of the flower garden in general.

Although flower gardens had not vanished with the advent of the landscape style, they were certainly in retreat. The abolition of formal, flower-filled parterres meant that flowers had to find refuge in a different kind of setting and again Dickie Bateman's garden at Old Windsor pointed the way. There, a rectangular enclosure with circular and rectangular beds cut into the turf was sited away from the house, while in another part of the garden there was a circular flowerbed in front of a classical

temple – a tableau similar to William Kent's in the garden of
Carlton House. Kent had in fact designed a flower garden for
Lady Burlington at Chiswick, which is but a variation of the one
at Kew. Both have architectural features, a central pond and
geometric beds, and are surrounded by trees and shrubbery. The
most famous flower garden of the century, however, was to be
laid out for George Harcourt, Viscount Nuneham, at Nuneham
Courtney in 1771; its beds were irregularly shaped but it was
still an enclosure in proximity to the house, near to the kitchen
garden and, as at Kew, close to the hot-house. It may well have
influenced royal Kew for it was begun during the lifetime of
Lord Nuneham's father, who was the Prince of Wales's gover-
nor and, in 1761, at the time when Kew was being laid out,
ambassador extraordinary for the marriage of the young King to
Princess Charlotte.

Augusta died on 8 February 1772, having spent the last nine
years of her life as a virtual recluse, dispensing even with the
customary rota of ladies-in-waiting and maids-of-honour. By the
summer of 1769 she was ill and began to reside solely in London, visiting Kew only twice a week. 'Reviled, traduced, hated,
she scarce dare appear out of her palace,' is how Walpole
unkindly winds up her life. Others dwelt on her many charities.

Augusta's Kew, however, was much admired, particularly in
France. Not only did the French study Chambers' book but, in
the aftermath of the peace of 1763, they could also come to
England to see what they were to interpret as *le jardin anglois-
chinois*. In 1770 F.J. Grosley, in his comprehensive guide to London, devoted more space to Kew than to any other garden and
told his French readers that at Kew could be found everything
that was richest and most varied in the new garden style, and
Madame Roland, visiting Kew in 1785, considered it 'the most
interesting [garden] that I have ever seen, the most skilful art
cannot be better disguised; everything breathes nature and free-
dom; everything is grand, noble and graceful'.

But Kew's future lay not in being a great royal garden but in
the extension of that small section devoted to exotic plants until
eventually the child was to swallow the mother. That legacy is
owed to Augusta and Bute who within five years of its creation
had established its botanical reputation. Peter Collinson, writing
in 1766 to his friend John Bartram of Philadelphia, perhaps the
principal source for new American plants and trees in England,
already judged Kew 'the Paradise of our world, where all plants
are found that money or interest can procure'. And so it has
remained to this day.

ROYAL BOTANIZING

QUEEN CHARLOTTE, WIFE OF GEORGE III

Charlotte of Mecklenburg-Strelitz (1744– 1818), unlike her two predecessors Caroline and Augusta, was always to be excluded from political affairs and as a result her garden-making was to take quite another direction. The eighth child and second surviving daughter of the ruler of an obscure North German state, Charlotte was the only royal princess who fitted the bill when the urgent search for a wife for George III began in 1761. The King had come to the throne in 1760, at the age of twenty-two, and both his mother and his chief minister, the Earl of Bute, wanted to distract him quickly from his desire to marry the beautiful Lady Sarah Lennox. It was stipulated that his bride was neither to have intellectual tastes nor show any disposition to engage in public affairs. As well as Protestant, she would also almost inevitably have to be German, because of George's Hanoverian blood, but of the few candidates of marriageable age, most were eliminated as being either deformed, having madness in the family or for being too intellectual. The eighteen-year-old Charlotte, unworldly and from a poverty-stricken principality that English critics soon

QUEEN CHARLOTTE IN 1771; A DETAIL FROM A PORTRAIT BY
Johann Zoffany. The vase of flowers at her elbow signals what was to
become her life's passion, the study of botany.

BUILT IN THE 1790s AS A LARGE GARDEN PAVILION, FROGMORE HOUSE,
near Windsor Castle, looks much as Queen Charlotte left it. Though
now glazed, what was the verandah looked out on to one of the
earliest gardens to be laid out in the new picturesque style with
winding walks and a meandering lake. Its basic structure remains
unchanged, although it was replanted in the Victorian period.

QUEEN CHARLOTTE'S COTTAGE AT KEW WAS BUILT IN ABOUT 1744. Two years earlier George III and Charlotte had inherited the Kew estate on the death of the King's mother, Augusta. Although it was by then an old-fashioned garden, they never altered it, Charlotte indeed finding her botanic interest quickened by the inheritance. The Queen's one addition was this deliberately picturesque cottage, built supposedly to a design of her own, in which the family could occasionally eat or even pass the day. The exterior was rustic while inside were two elaborately decorated rooms, an elegant print room with a pretty painted room above, as well as a kitchen and waiting rooms for servants which had a separate entrance. The cottage still stands in a quiet corner of Kew today (*opposite*).

The upper room (*above left*), now somewhat unsympathetically re-instated, was decorated as though it were a pergola with flowering climbers entwining wooden supporting poles. It is probably the work of one of Charlotte's daughters, Princess Elizabeth, and provides evidence of just the effects that would have been seen in the garden itself. Here (*above right*) we see two favourite late eighteenth-century climbers, brilliant blue ipomoea and scarlet nasturtiums.

dubbed as 'Muckleberry-Strawlitter', seemed the only suitable bride. The report on her ran: 'She is not a beauty but what is little inferior, she is *amiable*.' She spoke French well and excelled at music but knew little English.

The marriage took place in September 1761, amidst much good will for the popular young King and his new wife who was certainly no beauty but had a trim figure, pretty eyes and dark hair, albeit a flattened nose and too wide a mouth. From the outset Charlotte's role was circumscribed and apart from her official appearances on public occasions, such as the courts at St James's, she was to lead a cloistered existence. Her task was to be a child-bearer and between 1762 and 1783 she produced no less than fifteen children, thirteen of whom survived.

With Bute's political resignation in 1763 and Augusta's lessening hold on her son, George and Charlotte established their own secluded domestic life together and they set out to introduce all that was new in the 1760s into the royal gardens, a revolution epitomized by employing the man who so far had been spurned in royal circles, 'Capability' Brown. Up until the accession of the new King, Brown's connection with the Whigs had delayed his path to royal preferment, although he was at the height of his career and had already embarked on two of his most famous commissions, Chatsworth, in 1760 and Blenheim three years later. Brown has remained the most famous of all landscape or garden designers; his work is considered the climax of the English landscape style in which there is no trace of rigidity

BUCKINGHAM HOUSE HAD BEEN built in 1705 for the 1st Duke of Buckingham. An engraving by Sutton Nicholls of *c.*1731 shows the magnificent ironwork screens by Jean Tijou framing a *cour d'honneur* with an elaborate fountain at its centre (*right*). When the house was purchased by George III in 1761 as a dower residence for Charlotte and remodelled by Sir William Chambers in the 1760s, it assumed a more modest guise in keeping with the more domestic image of the consort of the monarch. In this detail of a view by William Westhall in the 1760s (*below*), it is enclosed by unpretentious railings while simple grass leads up to the walls of the house.

or formality. Kitchen and flower gardens were banished to some distant enclosure and the parkland was brought right up to the windows of the mansion, with breathtaking views created by the masterly handling of smooth gradients and magnificent lakes.

In July 1764 Brown was made Chief or Master Gardener at Hampton Court with a salary of £1107 6s a year, with an additional £100 for growing pineapples. Two years later St James's Park was added at an extra £40. In practice this meant that he received £2000 per annum for life, out of which he had to meet the expenses of the trees, plants and labour in the gardens under his control. In terms of cost the new style was dramatically cheaper than the old. 'Capability' Brown ran Hampton Court on £100; under William III in an average year it cost £4000. St James's is an even keener index: in about 1700 it cost just £500 per annum; under Brown this dropped to £40.

Brown and his family moved into Wilderness House at Hampton Court but although he is remembered for destroying some of the greatest baroque gardens in the country, he never touched Daniel Marot's masterpiece. Tradition has it that 'on being solicited by the King to improve the grounds . . . he declined the hopeless task, out of respect to himself and his profession'. In fact the impulse to alter the garden was not there, for after George II's death the court was never to reside at Hampton Court again and its future was to be that of grace and favour residences. By 1769 Brown was accused of neglecting the garden and the only surviving visible evidence of his work is the Great Vine. This was planted in 1768 and by the mid-Victorian period it was already a famous sight, covering 2300 square feet and producing some 2000 bunches of grapes.

When George III asked Brown to update Richmond Gardens in 1764 it was a defiant gesture in the face of his mother and Tory principles, for Brown's arch-rival was Sir William Chambers, designer of neighbouring Kew. Chambers never ceased to vilify Brown as an upstart peasant who dared trespass

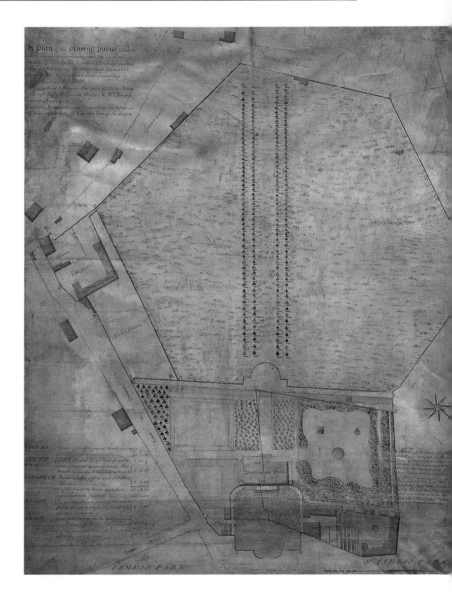

THE GARDENS OF BUCKINGHAM HOUSE HAD INITIALLY BEEN LAID OUT FOR the Duke of Buckingham by Henry Wise in the formal style, respecting the central axis and with attention to symmetry. By the time this plan was made in 1760 (*above*), alterations had taken place and more informal serpentine beds had been laid out in an area to the north of the house. The Royal Library contains later designs attributed to 'Capability' Brown which incorporate the forty acres which make up the present extent of the gardens. In this proposal (*right*) the formal lay-out was to be swept away in favour of a garden in the landscape style with sweeping expanses of grass enclosed by irregular groves of trees and winding walks, but also with a highly unusual oval lake in the style of Brown's contemporary, Thomas Wright.

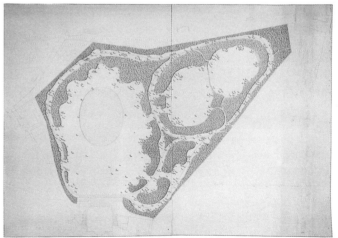

into his preserve. And nor was he the only critic, for in updating Richmond Brown swept away one of the greatest masterpieces of garden design in the early landscape style. William Mason's *An Heroic Epistle to Sir William Chambers* laments the barbarism of it all, attacking the 'untutored Brown' as a 'peasant' who had emerged from a 'melon-ground' and had levelled the 'wonders' created by 'good Queen Caroline'.

Brown turned Richmond into one large park, dispensing with the arable land which had been one of its most distinctive features and turning it into woodland. The only part of his scheme recognizable today is the Rhododendron Walk, whose structure though certainly not its planting remains as he left it. Otherwise Brown's Richmond went the way of Bridgeman's and Kent's. At the time, though, the young King and Queen took an intense interest in its creation and Brown's foreman, Michael Milliken, once wrote to his employer: 'Their Majesties came into the works on Saturday after you was gone . . . He

competition with Augusta's garden on the other side of Love Lane, for it studiously avoids any use of buildings at all. In the hierarchy of the royal works organization Brown was in fact subservient to Chambers and it was Chambers who was commissioned to design a new palace for Richmond in the midst of his rival's park. However, when Augusta died in 1772, George and Charlotte inherited Kew and the new Richmond Palace was never built. There was no attempt to sweep away his mother's extraordinary creation at Kew and indeed, unlike Richmond, it was said that nothing gave the Queen greater pleasure than 'beautifying and enriching' these gardens.

Charlotte's only addition to Kew was a cottage built, according to the *London Magazine* in 1774, to her own design. That is arguable but it is certainly very different from any previous royal garden building. In one way its precursor was Queen Caroline's dairy, which presupposes that she played the milkmaid. The idea of Charlotte's cottage seems to have been

said He had been detained but should see you next Saturday. The King did not bid me inform you so. But I do in case you should be engaged [so that] you can possibly put it off for that day as I think he rather wishes to see you. He was much pleased with the levels and asked if you was not so too. I told him you found no faults.'

In another letter, to his wife, Milliken reported that the royal couple used to come two or three times a week to inspect progress and spoke of their great enthusiasm for it.

Richmond can only have been embarked on in a spirit of

inspired by the French so-called *ferme ornée*, a cottage which from the outside looked suitably rustic but within was luxuriously fitted out. By the middle of the 1770s such cottages had become an independent element in any French picturesque garden and the Kew cottage, with its servants' quarters and richly appointed interior decoration, was built facing a paddock and the royal menagerie. In 1806 the menagerie was replaced with a flower garden and today the cottage can be seen in a remote glade at the end of a vista of rhododendrons.

Almost simultaneously with the remodelling of Richmond, designs were made for 'improving' the grounds of Buckingham House at the end of the Mall in London. George III had acquired this in 1761 for £28,000 as a dower home for the Queen but he himself quickly came to prefer it as his London place of residence instead of St James's. The house, much smaller than today's Buckingham Palace, had been built in 1705 for the 1st Duke of Buckingham and the garden was a grand formal one by Henry Wise, with a long rectangular canal and wilderness.

Nothing could have been more old-fashioned by 1760 and the

indications are that all of it was changed. The stately approach with ironwork screens by Jean Tijou and a huge courtyard with a fountain certainly vanished. The age of absolutism was past and the emphasis was now on approachability. Indeed George specified that it be called not a palace but 'The Queen's House'. Between 1762 and 1776 the building was remodelled by Chambers and the grounds were apparently also re-laid out. Two projected designs survive in the Royal Library. Although attributed to 'Capability' Brown, they closely resemble the highly individual response to the landscape style of Thomas Wright, a contemporary of Brown's, and an astronomer who advised on and designed over thirty major gardens.

At Buckingham House on 6 June 1763 a surprise fête was staged in honour of the King's birthday two days before. George was led to an upper room at the back of the house and the shutters were thrown open to 'a most surprising and entrancing spectacle'. The architect Robert Adam had transformed the garden: a temporary bridge had been constructed and also a huge classical exedra into which was set a series of transparencies lit by four thousand glass lamps. The central one depicted the King giving peace to every part of the globe (the terms of peace with France arranged at the close of 1762 were not finally proclaimed until March 1763) and trampling underfoot the hostile figures of Envy, Malice and Detraction.

George at this point had been on the throne less than three years and Bute had just ended his short-lived political premiership. Idolized by the young King even more than by Augusta, Bute doubtless helped form Charlotte's taste for botany, one which took a more dedicated and informed direction than that of her mother-in-law. After his resignation as prime minister in April 1763, Bute created a large botanical garden at his new country house, Luton Hoo, in Bedfordshire, and by the time of his death in 1792 he had become an important patron of the wave of botanical literature which marked the second half of the century. During these years he continued to have a powerful influence on royal garden-making, for Charlotte, like Augusta before her, shared and consulted with him as her interest in botany grew ever deeper.

Botanizing for Charlotte became an all-consuming pursuit, filling what would otherwise have been long empty days. It also brought her friendships, and indeed those with women of an older generation offered her a pattern upon whose activities she was to model her own life. One in particular was Margaret Harley, the Dowager Duchess of Portland, to whose house at Bulstrode, near Beaconsfield in Buckinghamshire, came the famous people of the age. The Duchess was a munificent patroness of the natural sciences and an avid collector: the Portland Museum was known throughout Europe and the sale of its contents after her death in 1785 lasted over a week. Among those she patronized was one of the most outstanding botanical artists of the century, Georg Dionysius Ehret, as well as the Rev. John Lightfoot, who dedicated his *Flora Scotica* of 1777 to her and whose famous herbarium George III later purchased for 100 guineas and presented to Charlotte. The Queen probably also owed her pioneer interest in the picturesque to the Duchess, who showed her the manuscript of William Gilpin's tour of the Lakes and Cumberland, a key influence on the picturesque movement and dedicated to the Duchess of Portland when it was published in 1786.

At Bulstrode, which was only about half an hour's journey from Windsor Castle for the royal family, Charlotte and George met Mary Grenville, Mrs Delany, in 1776 and immediately a friendship was struck. Mrs Delany, then in her mid-seventies and her second widowhood, epitomized the acme of those activities which filled the vacant hours of an eighteenth-century lady of the upper classes: paper-work, embroidery, drawing and shellwork. In 1772 she had hit on collage as a means of delineating the rapidly expanding range of plants pouring into the country from around the globe and during a period of a decade she delineated some thousand flowers, eighty-four of which are annotated on the reverse as

THE NEW BEDHANGINGS FOR QUEEN CHARLOTTE'S LODGINGS AT WINDSOR, which have been restored and are now on display at Hampton Court (*above*), were designed in 1778 by the acclaimed flower painter Mary Moser. The embroidery includes botanically accurate representations of hundreds of different flowers and reflects developments in botanic illustration at the end of the eighteenth century in which the Queen played an important role. The bed was said to have cost £14,000; an indication of how large a sum this was is given by the fact that Gainsborough, then at the height of his fame, charged 160 guineas for a full-length portrait.

having come from the Royal Botanic Gardens at Kew.

Both the King and the Queen, who were virtually half her age, came to adopt her as a kind of benign aunt. She was a woman whose gaiety, warmth and wit of observation shine through her letters, and she gives a lively account of one of the royal visits to Bulstrode in August 1778, describing how the King and Queen asked to see her collages. She placed the book on the table and they eagerly gathered around, the Queen from time to time asking questions about this or that particular flower. The King brought Mrs Delany a chair. 'Sit down, sit down,' said Charlotte, 'it is not everybody has a chair brought them by a king.'

By 1785, when Charlotte's friend and benefactress, the Duchess, died, Mrs Delany's sight was failing and she had had to give up her paper collage work. The King and Queen gave her a little house in Windsor, to which they often came, and provided her with an annuity of £300. She died at the then enormous age of eighty-eight and her portrait by John Opie was to hang in Queen Charlotte's bedchamber at Buckingham House.

A friend of even longer standing was Sir Joseph Banks, in terms of botanic endeavour the giant of the age. He was presented to Charlotte in 1771 and was to be central to the primacy of the Royal Botanic Gardens over the next decades. Spring Grove, Banks's house, was not far from Kew and the Queen was always a welcome guest. William Aiton, who had retained his position at Kew under George III, had been promoted to the management of the royal forcing and pleasure gardens where Charlotte had her own figgery, vinery, pinery, peach and cherry house.

Charlotte's passion for botany had an enormous influence on upper-class taste and set the seal on the role of what might be described as women in the garden. It was also a passion which steadily increased in almost exact inverse proportion to the state of her marriage. If her restricted role and early embittering experiences under her dominant mother-in-law had made botany a welcome escape, her horticultural interests became all-important with the onset of the King's illness in the late 1780s. George suffered from the inherited latent disease of porphyria, a metabolic disorder then not understood or treatable, which affects the central nervous system, and in his case resulted in bouts of increasingly prolonged madness. Charlotte, often living in fear of his irrational and sometimes violent behaviour and his ill-treatment of the children, was forced to create a separate life for both herself and her daughters, none of whom the King would allow to marry before the age of thirty.

George's first serious bout of insanity occurred in 1788–89, by which time Charlotte's taste for botany was already highly developed and she could write to Bute on 17 March 1788 offering him 'a sight of the beginning of an herbal from impressions on black paper'. The Queen, doubtless influenced by Mrs Delany, wanted to cut new ground by pressing not only leaves

CHARLOTTE CREATED HER AVANT-GARDE PICTURESQUE GARDEN AT FROGMORE in the 1790s as a place of solace from the progressive madness afflicting the King. It was a horticultural composition in terms of the Romantic age, an enchanted glade in the midst of an ancient forest with winding walks tracing a path through light and shade, evoking a succession of emotional moods from tranquillity to fear. The architect James Wyatt designed a gothick ruin clad in ivy to provide the Queen and her daughters with the kind of *frisson* we associate with the fashionable gothick novels of the era. The original intention of the ruins was still apparent in the first decade of the twentieth century before storms brought down the large old trees (*opposite below*); today, (*opposite above*) the effect has been lessened by concealing the ruin behind a splendid wisteria.

but 'the flowers and stalks, which I believe has not been done before with any success'. She worked on the project with her daughter, the Princess Royal, and with the assistance of the Royal Gardener, William Aiton, and the Swiss geologist, Jean André de Luc. It was a formidable task, beyond, as she explained, the physical resources of ladies: 'the specimens of plants being rather large it requires more strength than my arms will afford, but in the smaller kinds I constantly assist.'

Both the Queen and her daughters received botanical instruction from the President of the Linnean Society, Sir James Edward Smith, and drawing lessons from the renowned Franz Andreas Bauer, botanical painter to the royal garden at Kew. Dr Robert John Thornton, in his dedictation to Charlotte of his *New illustration of the sexual system of Linneaus* wrote: 'There is not a plant in the gardens at Kew (which contain all the choicest productions of the habitable globe) but has been drawn by her gracious Majesty, or some of the Princesses, with a grace and skill which reflect on these personages the highest honour.'

The evidence for that is still in the Royal Library at Windsor, although few drawings by Charlotte herself have ever been identified. One volume contains a series of large botanical drawings by the Princess Royal, dated from 1777 to 1784, some of which are copies from plates in John Miller's *Illustratio Systematis Sexualis Linnaei* (1777), but others are of plants and flowers drawn directly from life. Elizabeth, the third of Charlotte's six daughters, was genuinely talented; she drew and etched, designed fans, did paper-work and was capable of turning her hand to quite extensive decorative schemes. Flowers figured largely in all these designs and were used by her, for example, on the cotton velvet seat furniture at Buckingham House. She is the likely author, too, of those on the walls of the upper room in her mother's cottage at Kew. The most substantial body of her work, however, is still at Frogmore, her mother's house, where the 'long narrow room' recorded by the diarist Joseph Faringdon, has 'painted flowers, and subjects of children etc. cut in paper . . . They all show ingenuity.'

Frogmore indeed lies at the heart of Charlotte's botanizing. In

73

May 1790 she acquired a cottage and a garden there, on a site half a mile south-east of Windsor Castle on the other side of the main thoroughfare running from Old Windsor to London. It was renamed Amelia Cottage in honour of her youngest daughter and the architect James Wyatt was brought in to suggest improvements. It was never intended to be anything other than a garden building like the Kew cottage, a place where the Queen and her daughters could escape from the cold and rigours of the Castle and, as his madness and violence escalated, the King. Wyatt's initial proposal was to demolish the existing building and replace it with a fashionable *cottage orné* in the gothick style with four towers and 'a colonnade the whole length of the house which will make a sweet retirement in the summer all dressed out with flowers'. That, however, was considered too expensive and abandoned.

Then, two years later, the problem was solved when George bought Frogmore House for Charlotte. This small seventeenth-century country house built by Hugh May was transformed by Wyatt into a large pavilion. The transformation included the

colonnade which Charlotte had longed for (which is now glazed), at either end of which there were pavilions. Her only real extravagance was the Mary Moser Room, commissioned from the celebrated flower painter and founder member of the Royal Academy.

There was no tradition of flower painting in England and Mary Moser's career reflects the enormous interest in the subject which was such a feature of the late eighteenth century. Charlotte collected flower pictures by Mary Moser and the room, which reputedly cost £900, is a unique record of what was grown in the Queen's own flower garden at Frogmore. Although elements in the scheme may have been part of a design for the Audience Chamber at Windsor, the overall effect is of a floral pavilion held in by an azure sky, a room where even in winter the sky would be always blue and the flowers of summer at their zenith.

The Mary Moser Room is the clue to what must have been the most exciting feature of Frogmore and for the Queen, its *raison d'être*, the flower garden. Already in the autumn of 1790

she had begun to build a greenhouse among some old cabbages on the site of the kitchen garden, which she had determined to transform into a flower garden. On 20 November she wrote to Lady Harcourt of her preference for 'a cheerful well wooded country and the sweet odours of the flower garden'. Both the King and Queen were frequent visitors to the house of the 2nd Earl of Harcourt and his wife Elizabeth, Nuneham Courtenay, near Oxford, which had the most famous flower garden of the eighteenth century.

That had been laid out by the poet, cleric and landscape designer, William Mason, in 1771 for Lord Harcourt, then Lord Nuneham, and was a landmark in the cult of flowers as a reflection of human sensibility. Lord Harcourt, a Whig with strong republican leanings, was a fervent follower of Jean-Jacques Rousseau who propounded the view that man was at his best and purest in a state of nature. In his novel of 1761, *La Nouvelle Héloïse*, Rousseau describes a small garden that expressed his philosphy and Mason and Nuneham set out to create such a garden. It had winding walks, shady trees and

THE GROUNDS OF FROGMORE HOUSE WERE USED FOR A SERIES OF SUMMER fêtes to which Queen Charlotte invited several hundred guests at a time. There would be pavilions for supper, and what was called the barn, designed by one of her daughters, for dancing. But each occasion in addition called for an overlay of stage scenery to the garden. The most famous of these entertainments was given in 1809 and was designed to celebrate the imminent Jubilee of the King's accession and to pay tribute to British naval victories in the Napoleonic wars. The view here, a detail of a coloured engraving by Wyatt of 1809, is from the colonnade of the house from which the Queen made her entrance amidst a dazzling firework display which signalled the arrival on the water 'as it were by magic' of 'two triumphal cars drawn by two sea-horses each, one occupied by Neptune, and preceded by the other with a band of music'. Simultaneously sacrificers ascended to a Grecian temple Wyatt had designed on the island in which there was an illuminated transparency in which the Eye of Providence looked upon a portrait of the King. Incense arose from nine altars and the musicians struck up 'Rule Britannia'.

irregularly shaped flowerbeds edged with box but crammed with flowers that graduated in height from front to back. Mason's claim was to have brought both the 'poet's feeling and painter's eye' to the garden, creating a floral paradise and what would be recognized as the picturesque flower garden.

Although no picture exists of Charlotte's flower garden at Frogmore, it can only have been of this revolutionary kind, for it was laid out by Mason's curate, the Rev. Christopher Alderson, rector of Eckington in Derbyshire. She dated the creation of her 'little Paradise' to February 1791, when he began to lay out her flower garden, undertaking, as she wrote, 'to render this unpretty thing pretty'. The greenhouse built under the direction of William Aiton was completed in March and reckoned 'by all connoisseurs . . . to be very fine'. Soon afterwards plants arrived from Kew to stock the beds. 'My chief plants,' she told her son Augustus, 'are to be the natives of England and all such foreign ones as will thrive in our soil.' Among the lists of plants sent from Kew in November 1793 and March 1794 are shrubs such as hydrangeas, spireas, *Kalmia latifolia*, *Rhododendron ponticum*, *Daphne cneorum*, *Azalea nudiflora* [*Rhododendron periclymenoides*], *Magnolia glauca* [*M. virginiana*], *Clematis florida* [*C. f. bicolor*], and Botany Bay jasmine [probably *Jasminium suavissimum*], as well as sedums, saxifrages, violas, cyclamens, geraniums, hyacinths, anemones and ericas.

Charlotte's flower garden was, however, only one element in a garden which was thirteen acres in all; its basic landscaping can still be seen today, although overlaid by Victorian planting and the addition of royal graves and memorials. Alderson, in tandem with Charlotte's vice-chamberlain, Major William Price, converted the flat site into 'a pleasing diversity of mounts, glades, serpentine walks, and canals, with bridges, and other erections'.

William Price sometimes worked with his brother, Sir Uvedale Price, author of *Essays on the Picturesque* and creator of the prototype picturesque garden on his estate at Foxley in Herefordshire. Price's garden style rejected the work of 'Capability' Brown and that of his successor Humphry Repton, and advocated a return to painterly effects in the garden, but no longer inspired by the canvases of Claude Lorraine but of other Dutch, French or Italian painters. It was a style which also expressed current literary fashion, above all the rage for the gothick novel, with its long descriptions of remote and romantic glades set amidst primeval forests.

This is precisely how Frogmore, one of the earliest gardens laid out in the final phase of the landscape style, the picturesque, should be viewed. The glade was conceived as something highly cultivated and filled with exotic trees and shrubs, forming a startling contrast with the surrounding woods in which it was hidden. Such a garden was designed to play on the emotions, evoking moods ranging from melancholy to horror, through the manipulation of planting, changes of level, paths and buildings. Frogmore was described in the *Beauties of England and Wales*

of 1801 in a manner which captures for us how the visitor saw it at the time. It was 'a beautiful pleasure garden' that mysterious winding paths, shady shrubberies and a 'delapidated ruin and secluded temple' made 'peculiarly interesting'. It was also a hidden secret experience, 'the view of every distant object being excluded by trees and underwood'.

Like the grounds of Buckingham House, Frogmore could be transformed into a huge stage-set and from its completion in 1793 onwards it was the setting for a series of royal entertainments inaugurated, on 8 November 1793, with one to celebrate both Princess Augusta's birthday and the recent recovery from illness of Charlotte's daughter, Princess Sophia. On 19 May 1795, at a fête to mark Charlotte's birthday and that of the new Princess of Wales, sumptuous tents, decorated with a diamond design in red and white and which had belonged to Tipu, Sultan of Mysore, were set up on the lawn for the royal family to dine in. But the most famous entertainment was staged in 1809 for the imminent Jubilee of the King's accession, when a thousand guests including 'the town gentry and tradesmen, alike, clergy and all', were invited to Frogmore.

Tributes to Charlotte took less dramatic but more telling form in the many dedications to her of important botanical publications, among them Margaret Meen's *Exotic Plants from the Royal Gardens at Kew* (1790) and another volume of a similar kind, Francis Bauer's *Delineations of exotick plants cultivated in the Royal Garden at Kew* (1796); as Charles Abbot wrote in his famous *Flora Bedfordiensis* (1798), she had 'a genuine and ardent taste for the study of botany'.

She continued her interest up to the end of her life and on 13 August 1813 she is recorded going to visit her old gardening friend Sir Joseph Banks, by then in his seventies and chairbound. She returned twice more that year, when each time at lunch wonderful fruit from the garden would be served: peaches, plums, nectarines, apples, grapes and strawberries.

Five years later, on 17 November 1818, Charlotte died at Kew. She was seventy-four and her last view from her bedroom window was out on to her flower garden with the river beyond. After her death, to all intents and purposes Kew and its garden slept until her great-niece, Victoria, came to the throne. By then, under the aegis of a Royal Commission, Richmond Gardens and Kew were finally declared to be one, thus creating the Royal Botanic Gardens of today. They stand as much a monument to Charlotte as to her mother-in-law Augusta, and certainly no one would quarrel with Charles Abbot's tribute to her as 'the first female botanist in the wide circle of the British dominions'.

WYATT'S TEMPORARY PAGENT TEMPLE OF 1809 FOR QUEEN CHARLOTTE became a permanent reality half a century later when the tempietto for Queen Victoria's mother, the Duchess of Kent, was built in its place. It was designed in 1859, at the behest of Prince Albert and his mother-in-law, not only as a tomb but also to act as a summerhouse.

FASHION AND FORMALITY

GEORGE IV

The life of George IV (1762–1830) covers half a century of royal garden-making, from the time he came of age in 1783 to his death in 1830. As Prince of Wales, Regent and finally King, he was a compulsive builder, altering and remodelling a series of palaces, houses and gardens: Carlton House, Brighton Pavilion, Royal Lodge, Windsor Castle and Buckingham Palace, of which only the first is not still with us today. Not since Charles I had there been a king in whom exquisite taste and refined connoisseurship combined so potently. But his main passions were building and above all interior decoration. Gardens for George IV came a poor third.

That does not mean that his gardens were of no importance. They were rarely innovative but, like everything else about him from his carriages to the tie of his cravat, they were supremely fashionable. George IV approached the garden with the eye of a decorator bent on effect. His gardens, like the interiors of his houses, were stage-sets against which he moved, or rather displayed himself. He worshipped style and by the age of thirty he had already established himself as the unrivalled leader of

GEORGE IV AS REGENT; THIS DETAIL OF SIR THOMAS LAWRENCE'S BRAVURA oil sketch endows the Prince with all the high glamour to which he aspired. By 1814, the year that this was painted, the reality was already far different.

IN ITS FINAL EXOTIC GUISE BRIGHTON PAVILION, GEORGE IV'S EXTRAVAGANT seaside residence, was conceived by John Nash, who also designed the garden in the romantic picturesque vein. Irregular beds, thick set with evergreens, flowering shrubs, climbers, roses, herbaceous plants such as foxgloves and delphiniums, and infilled with colourful annuals, capture the Regency passion for a profusion of flowers.

CARLTON HOUSE ON THE MALL was the Prince's official London residence from 1783 until it was demolished in 1827. Under his aegis it was transformed into a setting of dazzling magnificence. The garden's prime function was to act as an arena for a long series of sumptuous alfresco fêtes, and in about 1803 Repton remodelled the garden both to ensure privacy by creating banks with shrubberies on the top along the Mall side and to accommodate, on large expanses of grass, the temporary tents and pavilions which catered for receptions of up to two thousand guests. He had presented his design (*left below*) in one of his customary watercolours in which a flap of paper could be lifted to reveal the proposed transformation. In typical Repton style a terrace, with a choice of either gothick or classical balustrading, was to lead to the garden.

A CAST-IRON CONSERVATORY (exterior *left above* and interior *opposite*), in the romantic gothick style, was added to Carlton House in about 1807, in spite of the fact that the house itself epitomized the acme of elegant neoclassicism. Modelled on Henry VII's chapel in Westminster Abbey, the conservatory – which led out of the dining room – was used for entertaining, on which occasions it was filled with flowers.

VIEW
FROM THE PRINCIPAL FLOOR OF
CARLETON-HOUSE
the foreground supposed a balcony in the style of the House, whether
COTHIC or GRECIAN &c

contemporary fashion. Homage was paid to his 'elegance of manners, his superb person, his exquisite taste in dress, as well as in the fitting out of his palaces, his equipages and entertaining'.

Unfortunately there was a canker within, for not only was he vain and open to flattery but prodigal on a reckless scale. At times his taste for splendour became so exaggerated that it tipped over into decadence. And this was during a period that saw the collapse of the *ancien régime* not only in France with the Revolution of 1789 but, with the subsequent Napoleonic Wars, in the rest of Europe too. Far from heeding the democratic impulses of his age (which in his youth he had embraced) George IV became more and more reactionary. This was reflected in his taste for collecting the art of pre-revolutionary France and in his building and gardening schemes, which revived styles of the vanished absolutist age. As a result he was wildly unpopular and the prestige of the monarchy was never to sink so low as during this prolonged rule of regal taste. George's response was not to curb any of his extravagances but to conceal them, hiding himself away in a series of private dreamworlds reminiscent of Ludwig of Bavaria. By the time that he succeeded as king in 1820 even his gardens were encircled by defensive earthworks designed to screen his by now florid and obese form from the gaze of his subjects.

George IV's garden-making was dominated by two people, the architect John Nash and the Royal Gardener, William Townsend Aiton, who were to carry through all his main creations. Aiton was the son of William Aiton who was in charge of the Royal Botanic Gardens at Kew. He succeeded his father there in 1793 and between 1810 and 1813 would bring out a revised edition of his father's work *Hortus Kewensis*, listing the enormous number of 11,000 varieties of plant by then grown at Kew, although in his later years Aiton was responsible for the shocking run-down of Kew which by the accession of Queen Victoria was a national scandal. In 1804 Aiton was one of the group who founded what became the Royal Horticultural Society. He had begun designing villa gardens in the 1790s and his obituary states that he 'made' the majority of George IV's. The word 'made' is perhaps indicative for the more significant role of design was assigned mainly to John Nash.

Nash is the architect most closely associated with the style of Regency England. The son of a millwright, he began his career in the office of the architect Sir Robert Taylor and from 1793 practised mainly in Wales as an architect of country houses. Through this he came to know the inventors of the picturesque style, Sir Uvedale Price and Richard Payne Knight. About 1795 he teamed up with the prime exponent of the picturesque in garden design, Humphry Repton, who had inherited the mantle of 'Capability' Brown. Repton reacted against Brown, gradually modifying the latter's compositions and transforming the estates of the landed gentry into a series of romantic pictures. He introduced terraces to divide the house from the garden and

developed the idea of separate gardens for different types of plants. His later work showed a marked antiquarian leaning, reviving formality from earlier centuries.

It was from Repton that Nash gained his knowledge about 'improving' the grounds of clients whose houses he designed, including those of George IV. His partnership with Repton broke down by 1802 but by then through Repton he had already met the Prince of Wales. The Prince would call on Repton for several of his projects but Nash became his favourite architect and it was Nash with Aiton who would finally carry through for the Prince his grandest metropolitan improvement, Regent's Park, as well as Windsor's Royal Lodge in its first phase, parts of Carlton House, Brighton Pavilion and finally what was to be Buckingham Palace. Sir John Summerson has written that there is 'a strong case for designating John Nash the greatest figure in the whole picturesque movement'. Nash was mainly responsible for the spread of gothick irregularity and the mania for vernacular cottage architecture, both of which were marked features of the picturesque movement in the decades after 1790.

The first project undertaken by the Prince of Wales was at

long liaison with Mrs Fitzherbert. He liked the little seaside town and in 1787 he commissioned Henry Holland to build a 'Marine Pavilion' for him. The Pavilion was an elegant building in the classical style with views to the sea, and what little garden there was Holland laid out with a large lawn and shrubs planted to conceal the adjacent Assembly Rooms. In 1795, when the Prince reluctantly married Caroline of Brunswick as the only means of clearing his debts, Holland was called on to enlarge and alter his original building and this time a garden was included in his groundplan. Holland was rarely interested in areas beyond those close to his buildings but he proposed a circular formal flower garden protected by a shrubbery. Within a year, however, the Prince's marriage to Caroline foundered irreparably, the couple thereafter living apart, and the alterations were never carried out.

In 1801 Holland prepared yet another scheme for the building, with a variant of the circular flower garden. But two years later the Prince had decided to go in a quite different direction, commissioning designs in the Chinese style not only from Holland but from a second architect, William Porden. Nothing materialized but it was decided to proceed that same year with a vast stable block in the Indian style by Porden, aptly known today as the Dome.

In all of these architectural transmutations the garden hardly figured until 1805 when the Prince summoned Humphry Repton. Repton had already been involved in improvements to the grounds between 1797 and 1802, for which he had received the sum of £264 in all. Since then the situation had changed considerably because in 1803 more land had been purchased to the west and permission gained to move the road on it.

They met on 24 November 1805 and in his autobiography Repton acknowledges 'the elegance and facility of the Prince's own invention, joined to a rapidity of conception, and correctness of taste, which I had never before witnessed'. The Prince, he records, had been delighted with examples of his work, particularly one in which 'you *dared* to make a perfectly straight gravel walk'. Repton and the Prince walked together in the Pavilion grounds where 'he talked as if he had never thought on any other subject but gardens, parks and landscapes'. When Repton asked him to explain his own ideas on the gardens of the Pavilion, the Prince replied: 'I confess I have never satisfied myself – nobody understands that the importance of a thing does not depend on its real but its apparent extent – in short I wish you to consider the subject well, and to give me your opinion unbiased by any thing you may have heard to be mine, or by any prevailing taste or fashion, by which the world is apt to be led.'

Three weeks later Repton made the first of a series of presentations of his designs, which were compiled in one of his famous Red Books (now in the Royal Library at Windsor) and would be published in 1808 when the project seemed likely to proceed. The Prince was enraptured: 'I consider the whole of this book as perfect! *I will have every part of it carried into immediate execution.*' Sadly, he did not. The project foundered on the expense of the war with France and the Prince's own mountain of debt. But the scheme of this great royal garden is one of breathtaking originality, totally fitted to the client's theatrical temperament.

Repton, realizing that it was impossible to conceal Porden's mammoth Indian stables, made them a point of departure for transforming both the Pavilion and garden into a Mogul fantasy. He had just been working on such an Indian garden for a retired nabob at Sezincote in Gloucestershire, for which Indian features had been designed by Thomas Daniell, author of the six-volume *Views of Oriental Scenery* (1795–1808). With this plus William Hodges' *Select Views of India* as his inspiration, Repton recommended transforming the Pavilion into a Regency Taj Mahal surrounded by a floral paradise. The garden on the west side was to be extended and enclosed with glazed corridors banked with flowers, providing a place to saunter and relax in the winter months. Responding to the Prince's leaning towards formality, the composition centred on a rectangular pool reflecting the stable block and emphasized by numerous domed minarets, pavilions, pierced screening and arcading in the Indian manner.

The garden on the east side, however, was to be Chinese in character. By 1800 reports had reached Europe of the gardens of the Cantonese merchants, which, unlike the Chinese gardens described by Sir William Chambers in the previous century, were not large and depended for their effect on exactly calculated detail. They used dwarf trees and plants, and small rock sculptures, together with climbers on trellis and containers perpetually filled with new flowers. As in the case of the Indian garden, Repton had recent experience of such a Chinese garden, having designed one at Woburn Abbey in 1804. He proposed a Chinese façade to the eastern face of the pavilion (not explaining how it could be reconciled with the Indian one) looking out on to a garden which was enclosed on three sides and had a lawn scattered with raised circular flowerbeds stocked with Chinese imports. To achieve his constant floriferous effect great use was to be made of bedding-out.

None of this great plan materialized and by 1814, when the Prince Regent finally decided to proceed with a scheme, it was one by Nash. Whereas Repton had linked house and garden in style, Nash's Mogul pavilion arose from a garden in which there was no attempt at a matching exoticism of design beyond the plants, which included ones from India and China. Those, however, were the responsibility of Aiton, whose planting lists still survive. For Nash, the acknowledged master of the picturesque, the ideal setting for his building was a garden in that style. The Pavilion, which in one sense is a stupendous garden building, had verandahs and no less than thirty-one french windows or floor-length sashes on the east front alone. Sweeping undulating lawns with winding paths and irregularly shaped shrub beds and borders were planted on picturesque principles, with a core

THE REBUILDING OF THE PAVILION at Brighton actually proceeded in the Indian style after George became Regent in 1811 but under the aegis of the Prince's favourite architect, John Nash. Nash designed the garden with William Aiton but in a far less imaginative way than Repton's amazing proposals of 1805. Instead it was to be a typical picturesque composition with a series of meandering walks from which the exotic building could be seen against irregular island beds. These were to be filled with evergreen and deciduous shrubs and trees, climbers, and quantities of colourful bulbous, herbaceous and bedding-out plants. Nash's own view of the west front (*below*), his groundplan and Aiton's original plant lists are being used to restore the west front garden today (*above*).

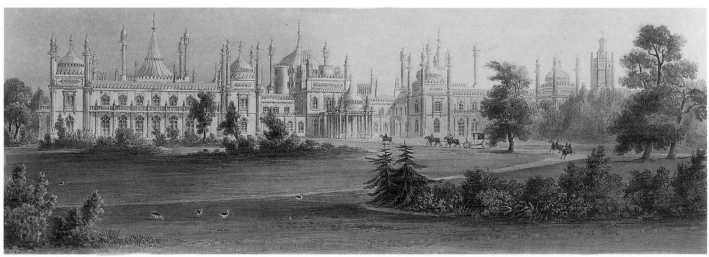

OF ALL GEORGE IV'S BUILDING EXTRAVAGANZAS, ROYAL LODGE IN WINDSOR Great Park was to be the target of the bitterest political satire. Here, hidden from his hostile subjects, it was thought that George connived with reactionaries and was ruthlessly exploited by the family of his last mistress, Lady Conyngham. In this cartoon by William Heath of 1824 the King rests on his spade while the Conyngham family garden. It also gives a rare glimpse of this so-called cottage with its large conservatory and records an early watering device.

ROYAL LODGE WAS A *COTTAGE ORNÉ*, AN ARCHITECTURAL EXPRESSION OF THE yearnings of the upper classes for the 'simple life'. Begun in 1813 as a temporary residence for the Prince Regent, it was vastly expanded in the 1820s. The garden and its planting played a role in concealing its size: a coloured engraving of the entrance dated 1824 (*opposite*) shows a modest, cottage-style country house with mullioned bay windows and an arch of honeysuckle over the door; but a screen of trees hides the truth, for above them arises a forest of Tudor chimneys.

of evergreens such as fir trees, Portugal laurel, holly and yew at the centre. A huge variety of plants – flowering shrubs, bulbs and perennials – filled the surrounding spaces and any gaps were made good by annuals and by flowers in pots. Great emphasis was laid on prolonging the flowering season and also on the use of climbers, which scrambled up trees and through the evergreens. Flowers such as foxgloves, poppies, pinks, lilies of all kinds, peonies, columbines, stocks, sweet williams and the new China roses would have followed narcissi, polyanthus, lily of the valley, primroses, wallflowers, tulips and daisies.

The Prince's third garden, at Royal Lodge, arose out of a political dilemma. In 1811, when George became Regent, he needed a house within easy reach of both Windsor Castle and London. There was no question of residing in the castle, which was already over-populated with the demented King, the Queen and five of his unmarried sisters. However, four miles south of the castle lay two eighteenth-century houses, the official residence of the Ranger, Great Lodge, and a second Lower Lodge, which the Regent took over. Nash was called on to replace the

latter with a small residence in the latest style, a *cottage orné*, which was begun in 1813.

The *cottage orné* evolved partly out of the type of garden building which Queen Charlotte had erected at Kew but which was now developed to a full-blown residence. Such buildings embodied aristocratic yearnings for the simple life away from the draughty grandeur of the great house and were seen as especially appropriate to men of taste and discernment, providing ideal settings for conversing with friends, communing with nature and study. The demand for gardens to complement the cottages coincided with the revival of the flower garden; flower-beds began to be sited close to the house, particularly where french windows could be thrown open to allow the full enjoyment of both blossom and scent. The new phenomena of the verandah and the conservatory offered transition points between house and garden. The verandah provided shelter in which to sit and a space for container plants, as well as having pillars and arches up which to train sweet-smelling climbers, while the conservatory ensured summer in winter.

These features of Regency gardening were incorporated in what began life as The Cottage and ended as Royal Lodge. The building went up so quickly that in 1815 the Prince was able to use it for the first time for Ascot week. By then no less than £52,000 had been spent and more was to follow after George III's death in 1820 when another, lesser architect, Jeffry Wyatt, later Sir Jeffry Wyatville, enlarged it. The final bill for what had begun as a temporary *pied à terre* was some £60,000 but, like everything else to do with George IV, its atmosphere and sense of style were unique. Sir Walter Scott visited it on 20 October 1826 and described it as 'a kind of cottage, too large perhaps for the style, but yet so managed that in the walks you only see parts of it at once, and these well composed, and grouping with the immense trees'.

Nash together with Aiton carried out the work on the garden and the landscaping, whose prime objective was to achieve an optical illusion that despite its rambling size Royal Lodge was a cottage. Large fastigiate trees interrupted what was in fact a very long façade. A verandah was added, its supporting pillars smothered with honeysuckle, and a conservatory, which screened the domestic offices. As at Carlton House, the conservatory was of cast iron with 'trellised pilasters' and a 'trellised temple' in the middle, all painted green. Inside, exotic birds flew around.

Further elaboration of the grounds followed in time for Ascot in 1821. On 2 April the *Reading Mercury* recorded: 'A covered walk, in a serpentine form, leading from the conservatory into the grounds for the convenience of his Majesty and his visitors during wet weather, is intended to contain all the rare shrubs, flowers and creeping plants that can be collected.'

This sounds exactly like Repton's proposals for Brighton, a corridor conservatory banked with blossom, and had it survived, Royal Lodge would perhaps have been as great a curiosity as the famous Pavilion. Those privileged enough to stay as guests would have sauntered out of the french windows on to the verandah terraces, the air heady with the fragrance of the honeysuckle, while before them stretched swaths of verdant lawn, majestic trees with climbers around their trunks, winding

CREATED IN 1749, VIRGINIA Water in Windsor Great Park was the largest artificial lake of its day (*opposite*). Under George IV it was used as the setting for his alfresco pleasures. Reached only by hidden and secret paths from Royal Lodge, it became the backdrop for a fantastic *ville imaginaire* in which the King and his guests could amuse themselves. The focal point of the diversions was the chinoiserie Fishing Temple. A coloured engraving of 1827 by W. Daniel (*above*) captures something of its delicate flamboyance, and depicts the nearby boat house and richly decorated supper tents with gilded crescent moon finials. Behind the Fishing Temple was a small decorative garden; its central round basin with a single fountain jet was surrounded by little stone urns on low plinths, while shrubs and small trees, some in containers, were dotted over the grass.

paths and flowerbeds edged in metal hoops to resemble large baskets brimming with flowers. *The Gardener's Chronicle* in 1828 gives a lively impression of just how remarkable the garden was. The cottage 'stands in an open forest glade, which has been polished by art, and ornamented with numerous masses, patches, groups of exotics, and scattered roses and flowering plants'. Those exotics would largely have been American ever-greens, in particular pines. Besides being rare they provided screening from the outside world, which was becoming an obsession with George IV.

The impact of Royal Lodge on arrival must have been quite extraordinary, for the approach was through densely planted woodland and circuitous paths that gave no hint of the fairytale floral paradise concealed within. Even after most of the Lodge had been demolished the garden lingered on. In 1837, the year of her accession, Queen Victoria recorded how she had gone 'all over the house and into the garden, which was in great beauty, full of flowers. It was so pretty and peaceful.'

However, Royal Lodge, more than any other of George's extravagances, came to symbolize in the public mind everything that made the King unpopular. The so-called 'Cottage clique', a group that included Princess Lieven, Prince Esterhazy and the Prince de Polignac, were all regarded as reactionary and anti-liberal in an age of fast-moving reform. The Princess gives a vivid picture of the indolent time they spent there: 'The site is pretty, fine, superb trees, very picturesque glimpses of the land-scape, a charming place. We had a lazy and very agreeable life there, always in the King's society. Many promenades in the forest, on the lake, sometimes dinners under tents, always music in the evening.' She got up at nine, lingered in the garden until

THE MAN-MADE CASCADE AT VIRGINIA WATER WAS CONSTRUCTED IN THE 1750s for George IV's uncle, the Duke of Cumberland, to disguise the dam which holds back the waters of the lake. It is perhaps one of the earliest examples of the deliberate creation of what was meant to pass as a natural phenomenon. It is a precursor of the garden tableaux favoured by the Picturesque Movement at the close of the century.

eleven, then dressed for luncheon with the King and went for a drive or boated on the river, returning in time to change for dinner.

Royal Lodge was the inner sanctum of what was a private arcadia on a stupendous scale, for the King in his obsession for privacy closed Windsor Great Park to the public. Not for the first time he became the butt of the caricaturist, William Heath, who depicted the ample form of George's last mistress Lady Conyngham pulling a child's walking frame that supported the obese figure of the King past a signpost to Virginia Water – the immense lake to the south-east of the Park. The King's fear of being seen by any prying eyes had reached manic proportions and in 1827 a visiting German Prince wrote that 'As soon as he rides out, the private part of the grounds is hermetically concealed to everyone without exception who does not belong to his own invited company.' He goes on to describe how the planting was thick 'for further security' and in areas where even a glimpse would be possible, three fences had been erected, one behind the other. Today the routes to and around Virginia Water still have some of that character of sylvan tunnels through which carriages could rumble unseen to the lakeside.

Virginia Water had been laid out in 1749 by Thomas Sandby for the King's uncle, William Augustus, Duke of Cumberland. It was the largest artificial lake of its day in the country, two miles in length, and Cumberland had added to it a number of decorative features. A fifty-ton hulk fitted up to look like a 'Mandarin Yacht' floated on the water, complemented by a chinoiserie pavilion on the lakeside. A triangular gothick belvedere, constructed by Henry Flitcroft, overlooked the lake from a hill to the south and an unprecedented 150-foot single-arch palladian bridge spanned the water, which was held in by a dam that was made into one of the earliest examples of a cascade with natural rockwork.

George IV used this inheritance as a basis upon which to conjure up a fantasy world, as though the exoticism of Brighton had been transferred to Virginia Water. The *raison d'être* for this pleasure complex was the King's love of fishing. Indeed his fishing rod survives and, like everything else connected with him, is beautifully decorated, with engraved gilt mounts and an absurdly large bejewelled fly. This sporting passion became the excuse to build a Fishing Temple, on which some £15,000 had been expended by 1828. In a letter to her son of 8 August 1826, Lady Holland describes it as 'in the Chinese taste, full of gilt dragons for ornaments: rather too expensive, *on dit*, considering Windsor, Buckingham House, and the state of the country'.

The construction was undertaken by Wyatville, although the design seems to have been the result of a combination of talents. *The Observer* reported in 1827 that the temple was 'from a pure and chaste design made by [the King] himself. The decorative part is given to Mr Crace.' Frederick Crace's firm was responsible for the interior decoration of Brighton Pavilion; a number of drawings for the project survive from his office and he sat for his portrait holding a design for the temple.

It was a fantastic building, one of a series which signalled the swansong of chinoiserie in the garden. Brightly painted in crimsons, blues and greens, with an abundant use of gold that caught the light, the Fishing Temple was a delicate, airy structure with staircases leading down to the waterside and walls made up of pierced screens. It was covered in multicoloured dragons, so many of them that one wonders whether this could explain the fate of those which once adorned the King's grandmother's pagoda at Kew. Inside, the temple was filled with furniture upholstered in green chintz 'sprinkled with marine productions', and outside at the back was a circular formal flower garden. Close by on the shore was an encampment of eight tents, four large and four small, erected by the army at a cost of £3170.

If one side of the lake was dedicated to Oriental fantasy, the other paid homage to imperial Rome. There, in 1826, Wyatville, with the aid of a detachment of the Royal Engineers, reconstructed a vast ruined temple using remains brought from Leptis Magna, a Roman city in the Libyan desert. Colonel Hanmer Warrington had persuaded the local North African ruler to offer

PARTS OF THE RUINS OF THE
Roman city of Leptis Magna in
North Africa, which had been
presented to the King as a gift,
were rearranged in 1826 on the
shore of Virginia Water
opposite the Fishing Temple to
create a triumphal tableau.
This incorporated a viaduct for
the one road through the park
which George IV could not
close to the public. The pencil
sketch by William Delamotte
of 1836 (*right*) shows how
quickly it began to be
neglected, but even in its
vandalized state today (*above*),
it remains the largest classical
garden ruin ever to be erected
in this country.

a choice of the city's remains to the Regent in 1816 and the principal basilica, a triumphal arch, a circus, a peristylum, an arcade and several other structures were excavated. The plundered pieces eventually reached England in March 1818, when they were presented to the British Museum where they languished until 1824 when the King suddenly sent for them.

The so-called Temple of Augustus formed by Wyatville provided a theatrical setting for the King on a grand scale. The public road running east-west was converted into a triumphal arch that acted as a proscenium spanning a path which went north-south through the huge ruin. From the lake two rows of columns, one set back from the other, emphasized the perspective while through the arch there was a semicircular pillared exedra with an altar. To this were added classical and later-period statues from various sources and a suitably monumental frame was provided by magnificent cedars, handsome beeches and willowy birches, the whole making up an unforgettable garden tableau. Even today the Leptis Magna ruins still form the largest artificial ruin ever constructed in this country, though they are a pale reflection of their former glory.

Life around the lakeside was one prolonged *fête champêtre*. On the lake floated a miniature man-of-war called the *Victorine*, which fired a salute on special occasions, when the band would also strike up 'God save the King'. Cumberland's Mandarin Yacht was to hand for expeditions and dinner was served either in the Temple or in one of the tents, when the party was serenaded by musicians from boats floating on the lake. When the King's seven-year-old niece, the future Queen Victoria, visited in 1826, she summed up the scene exactly: 'there was a large barge and everyone went on board and fished, while a band played on another!' Later her uncle took her to the Sandpit Gate where she was shown his private zoo. This included a splendid range of animals, from monkeys, gnus, elks and kangaroos to Mandarin horses, Brahmin bulls, a zebra, a leopard, a llama and a giant tortoise, plus an array of exotic birds – among them ostriches, parrots, eagles, Chinese partridges, wild Siberian swans and Greenland geese.

Royal Lodge and Virginia Water formed a base from which the King could supervise his transformation of Windsor Castle, for which Parliament had granted £150,000 in 1824 to repair and remodel. The proposals by Wyatville were used to turn the castle into the picturesque pile we know today, a monument to the romantic revival. This architectural treatment also affected the garden style.

Windsor Castle had no garden and the idea of making one on the eastern side seems to have first been put to the King by Charles Long, Lord Farnborough; a paper to this effect, probably in Farnborough's hand, is now in the Royal Library. Farnborough, a Trustee of the British Museum and one of the original Trustees of the National Gallery, was a person 'of considerable taste and accomplishment in painting . . . [he] has been called the Vitruvius of the present age'. His project shows a geometric

quartered flower garden with a fountain at its centre, surrounded on three sides by raised pergola-shaded walks and with a pair of steps leading from the east terrace past the garden's major focal point, 'the magnificent Vase now executing by Mr Westmacott'. This is the Waterloo Vase carved by Sir Richard Westmacott from a block of marble which had been presented by the Grand Duke of Tuscany to the Prince Regent to commemorate the battle of Waterloo; it is now in the grounds of Buckingham Palace. Although Farnborough's scheme was not carried out, it was his idea that a garden was needed and that, like the castle, its design should be of an antiquarian nature.

The creation of the East Garden entailed massive earthworks by Wyatville, making an irregular hexagonal enclosure with a battlemented terrace looking down on to a formal and symmetrical garden by William Aiton. Within an overall horseshoe shape, the area was quartered, with a fountain at the centre of a pattern of flowerbeds. The style of the garden reflected contemporary trends, for the formality of Repton's late work was an

WHEN WINDSOR CASTLE BEGAN TO be remodelled by Wyatville in 1824 a garden was added to the east beneath the King's private apartments (*above*). Like all the King's gardens it was designed to conceal him, and was enclosed by steep banks and walls. Under Queen Victoria a new entrance was made and the garden was opened to the public for the first time on particular occasions, as shown in this watercolour by Joseph Nash of 1844 (*left*).

WILLIAM AITON'S DESIGN FOR THE FLOWER GARDEN ON THE EAST TERRACE AT Windsor (*below*) looked to the past for its inspiration, to the formal parterres of the *ancien régime*. Highly criticized at the time, the lay-out remained virtually unchanged until as late as 1953 (*left*). It is now a simple, labour-saving rose garden (*above*).

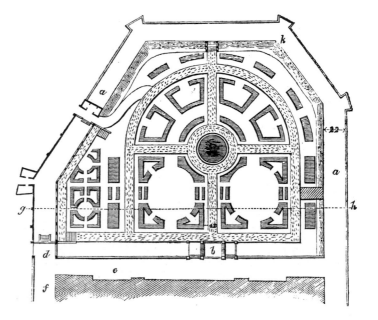

THE EAST TERRACE GARDEN UNDER GEORGE IV SIGNALLED A RETURN TO THE use of sculpture in quantity in the garden. Virtually all the major garden pieces commissioned or acquired by his predecessors were placed here in addition to those he collected himself which included a cast of the celebrated antique known as the Warwick Vase (*above*).

THE URN, SEEN (*above*) IN *c*.1907 WHEN IT WAS STILL AT WINDSOR, IS ONE OF A pair made in the 1690s for William III's garden at Hampton Court (and is now in the Orangery at Kensington). Sculpted by Edward Pierce, it depicts Meleager hunting the Calydonian Boar.

THE STATUE OF HERCULES AND THE LION (*left*) IS ONE OF FOUR CASTS OF Roman antiques made by Hubert Le Sueur in the 1630s for Charles I's garden at St James's Palace.

THE VASE (*far left*) MADE BY WILLIAM VAN MIERIS IN THE EARLY EIGHTEENTH century, is one of four bought by George IV in 1825.

established fact by 1822 when John Claudius Loudon published his *Encyclopaedia of Gardening*, the gardening bible of the times, in which all flower gardens were geometric.

Within the enclosure George IV assembled a remarkable collection of garden sculpture, which is still largely there today. Chief amongst this collection were the earliest reproductions of antique classical statues ever to be used in an English royal garden, the bronzes by the French sculptor, Hubert Le Sueur. These had been made after Charles I had sent Le Sueur to Italy to bring back 'the moulds and patterns of certain figures and antiques there', and were sited in the garden of St James's Palace, though some of them were later moved by William III to adorn the Fountain Garden at Hampton Court. The four in the Windsor East Terrace Garden are the Borghese Warrior, the Belvedere Antinous, the Diana of Versailles and the Hercules and the Telephus of the Vatican. To these George IV added, among others, a handsome bronze cast of the famous Warwick Vase and four superb early eighteenth-century urns by Willem van Mieris, made originally for a garden in Leiden and purchased by the King in 1825. There were also the two elaborate urns, carved by Caius Gabriel Cibber and Edward Pierce in 1692 for William III's Privy Garden at Hampton Court, and the superb series of statues by Francavilla which George's grandfather, Frederick, Prince of Wales, had purchased for his garden

at Kew but never lived to see put in place there. Finally there was a fountain by Bosio of Hercules and Achelous (which was presented to Kew Gardens in 1963 and is now in the centre of the Palm House Pond). George IV thus returned sculpture to the garden in a way not seen since the baroque age.

At the time derision was heaped on this garden. The orangery, sited in a 'ditch', was 'deforming'. As for Aiton's flower garden, 'the beds . . . are altogether too simple, or rather too poor in their outlines for the architecture of the castle'. Worse, there was no connection at all between the geometry of the layout and the architecture of the castle and it could not be discovered 'whether it was Sir Jeffry Wyatville or Mr Aiton' who had designed them. The planting 'we pronounce with confidence', the diatribe runs on, 'to be as far behind the present state of science in this branch of gardening, as the plan is deficient in those of design and taste'. In the process of this massive indictment we are told what the planting was: a mixture of rhododendrons, azaleas, kalmias, evergreen American shrubs, lilacs, standard roses and flowers. The writer placed it correctly in context as relating to 'the remains of parterres still existing in France' after the Revolution. Today both the original lay-out and complex planting have gone in favour of simple beds block-planted with roses.

George IV also added a focal point to the two-and-a-half-mile

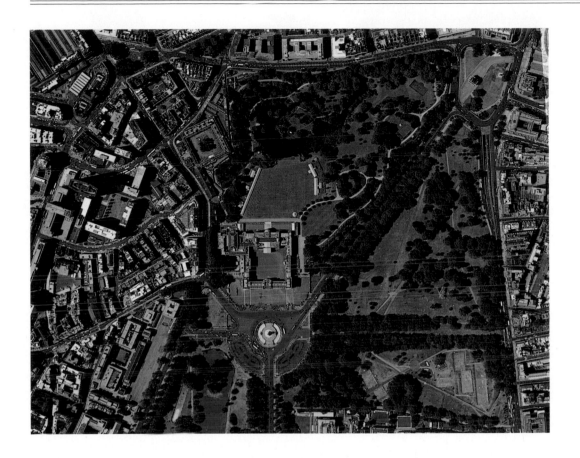

THE FORTY-ACRE GARDENS OF what was to become Buckingham Palace were re-landscaped after George IV's accession in 1820 under the aegis of Aiton, who was still working on it when Victoria came to the throne in 1837. The basic structure seen in Aiton's groundplan (*below*) remains remarkably untouched. A wide terrace leads to an expanse of grass, huge enough to entertain hundreds of guests. Indeed, the view from the air (*left*) shows the lawns dotted with tents and tables put up for the present Queen's summer garden parties. The lawns sweep down to a lake, made roughly in the shape of a question mark. The enclosing walls and banks planted with shrubs and trees were designed to provide privacy.

ST JAMES'S PARK WAS re-landscaped at the same time as the new gardens at the back of Buckingham Palace were being laid out to provide a picturesque foreground to the palace. The watercolour (*opposite*) by Joseph Nash of 1848 includes the triumphal gateway which was moved to Marble Arch when the east wing, which gave the palace the façade by which it is most easily recognized today, was added. The archway was to have been topped by the sculpture of George IV which is now in Trafalgar Square.

OVERLEAF: PATHS ALONG THE perimeters of Buckingham Palace gardens continue to give picturesque views of the palace across the water.

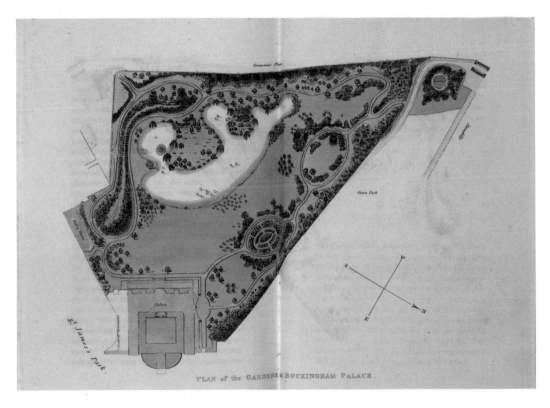

PLAN of the GARDENS of BUCKINGHAM PALACE.

Long Walk which had been planted a century and a half earlier by Charles II but which had led nowhere. The alterations to the castle created a splendid new gateway on the south side, leading out of Sovereign's Court directly on to the walk, and the King commissioned Westmacott to sculpt an over-life-size equestrian statue of his father to complete England's grandest garden vista. Known as the Copper Horse, the statue alone is twenty-seven feet high, weighing twenty-five tons, and it sits on an equally high pedestal consisting of huge boulders of rock over a brick foundation. Although commissioned during the King's lifetime, this statue was not finally put in place until after his death when, in October 1831, it arrived in pieces by cart.

The transformation of Windsor Castle went hand in hand with the rebuilding of what was to become Buckingham Palace. Nash was commissioned to convert Buckingham House and work began in 1825 but ran into severe difficulties three years later when faults in the construction were found to be so great that what had been built had to be demolished and rebuilt. The palace remained unfinished on George IV's death in January 1830 and his brother, William IV, brought in Edward Blore to complete it but it was not until the accession of Queen Victoria that the decision was finally made to make it the royal family's metropolitan palace.

As at Brighton, Nash seems to have worked in tandem with Aiton on the gardens, which show that extreme desire for privacy common to all the King's later projects. The earth excavated to make the new lake was used to form banks not only to conceal the royal stables but also parts of the garden itself. Exterior walls were built and in places supported the banks, on

top of which were planted trees and shrubs – a reworking of what had been done at Carlton House by Repton at the beginning of the century. The result was a picturesque landscape garden with outer perimeter walks which afforded glimpses of the impressive west façade of the palace. A wide terrace separated the building from the garden and was decorated with several vases and urns designed by Westmacott and made of Coadstone, a patented form of reconstituted stone. There was a flower garden and mixed borders which would have been crammed with a variety of flowers like those at the Pavilion; splendid specimen trees were also planted, many of which were standing until the great gale of 1987. The main feature of the garden, however, was grass, for the Buckingham Palace gardens were thought of as a setting for entertainments for hundreds of guests. They were, however, not to fulfil the role George IV conceived for them until the development of the royal garden party during Victoria's reign.

St James's Park and the Mall were also re-landscaped by Nash and Aiton to give the east front of Buckingham Palace a fitting setting. This area, which Nash was commissioned to redesign in 1827, still retained its Restoration period structure. Recalling, it seems, an unexecuted design by 'Capability' Brown, Nash transformed the park's rectangular canal into a serpentine lake with islands and around it created the gently undulating picturesque landscape with groves and clumps of trees and shrubs that it still retains. However, in contrast to Buckingham Palace, the enclosing walls were demolished and St James's became the first public royal park from which no one was to be excluded. The Mall, formerly a shaded avenue in which to stroll, now became primarily a carriage road, establishing it as the grand axial route to the new palace, although it was not until 1913 that the Admiralty Arch leading into Trafalgar Square gave the Mall its present significance.

Three years after the King's death the Duke of Wellington was riding along Virginia Water and galloped past the 'skeletons of the tents' near the Fishing Temple, a sight which made him 'quite unhappy'. 'Alas,' he said, 'the poor King! Many a day have I passed in those tents!' The anecdote signals the dissolution of George IV's horticultural achievements. Even by then the tents were clearly in ruins and the Fishing Temple, which can never have been very substantial, was under repair in 1850 and by the end of the century had vanished. This was the fate shared by many of the King's garden projects. Carlton House had already been demolished in 1827 and the Duke of York's Steps were built on the site of its garden. The garden at Royal Lodge did not survive long into Victoria's reign, the cottage itself being immediately demolished, and Brighton Pavilion (although plans exist today to restore the garden) slipped into royal oblivion when Victoria and Albert purchased Osborne in 1845. Today only St James's Park, Buckingham Palace and the East Terrace at Windsor Castle remain to remind us of George IV's massive contribution to royal garden-making.

DESIGNED IN THE 1820s, THE west façade of Buckingham Palace (*above*) and the balustraded terrace (*below*) look out over the gardens. The urns and vase, designed by Sir Richard Westmacott, add a note of regal flamboyance typical of George IV.

OVER FIFTEEN FEET HIGH, THE Waterloo Vase (*opposite*) was carved by Westmacott from a block of marble given to the Prince Regent by the Duke of Tuscany in gratitude for Britain's defeat of Napoleon. It was put in its present place in the grounds of Buckingham Palace in 1906.

TASTE AND MEMORY

QUEEN VICTORIA AND PRINCE ALBERT

Victoria (1819–1901) came to the throne almost by accident. George IV's only child, Princess Charlotte, had died in 1813, precipitating a crisis over the royal succession. The King's brothers were forced to discard their mistresses and marry, but it was only the Duke of Kent who produced a surviving child. On her accession in 1837 no one, however, could have foretold that this high-spirited young woman with memories of the extravagances of her 'Uncle King' would become the dutiful, almost puritanical matriarch who was to symbolize an age and give her name to its style in every form around the world, including that of the garden. The key influence in all this was Victoria's husband, Albert of Saxe-Coburg-Gotha (1819–61), whom she married in 1840. In the decade and a half from 1845 to 1860 they were constantly involved in one garden project or another, chiefly in the making of two new gardens, at Osborne on the Isle of Wight and Balmoral Castle in Aberdeenshire. Although Victoria took great delight in her gardens, it was Albert who was the creative force behind them, designing and working on them himself, and on his death in

THE DOMESTIC IDYLL OF VICTORIA AND ALBERT'S MARRIED LIFE IS
evoked in this detail from Sir Edwin Landseer's painting of 1840,
Windsor Castle in Modern Times.

THE BALMORAL ESTATE IN SCOTLAND WAS ACQUIRED IN 1852 AND WORK ON
building the new castle began immediately. Albert supervised every
detail of both castle and grounds, for there was little actual garden.
The environs were planted as though his native Thuringia in Germany
had been translated to the banks of the Dee. The area with flower
borders to the left of the glasshouses was added in the 1920s under
the aegis of Queen Mary.

1861 they would assume the status of shrines for the inconsolable Victoria, who would keep them unchanged throughout her long widowhood.

When Victoria succeeded her uncle, William IV, she was the first monarch to inherit the royal palaces and gardens as effectively a tenant in government-funded and -controlled buildings. For the first time a clear distinction was made between the official gardens of the Crown, which were the responsibility of the state, and the private gardens personally maintained by the monarch. Parliamentary accountability was henceforth to be a major consideration. As the century progressed the great private gardens of Victoria's predecessors, Kew, St James's, Hampton Court and Kensington Gardens, all became public, leaving only Buckingham Palace and parts of Windsor such as Frogmore as private to the monarch. Victoria's journals, which she kept all her life, are full of the miseries of dealing with the Department of Woods and Forests over the upkeep of the royal gardens. Partly as a consequence, and in startling contrast to the major

garden works constantly in train under George IV, as Prince, Regent and King, Victoria and Albert's building and garden-making initiatives were largely to be confined to their two private residences, Osborne and Balmoral, which were paid for solely from their own private fortunes administered by the Privy Purse over which the government had no control.

The royal gardens were in such a bad state in 1837 that they were the subject of heated public debate. Fourteen weeks after Victoria's accession the *Gardener's Gazette* made a savage attack on the state of Kew: 'slovenly and discreditable, and that of the plants disgracefully dirty'. The object of this onslaught was the Royal Gardener, William Townsend Aiton, then over seventy. He was defended by the formidable figure of John Claudius Loudon, the inventor of popular gardening, who eulogized Aiton's work at Buckingham Palace, then still in train. These exchanges unleashed a bitter war of words which partly contributed to the setting up of an official committee of inquiry into the state of the royal gardens.

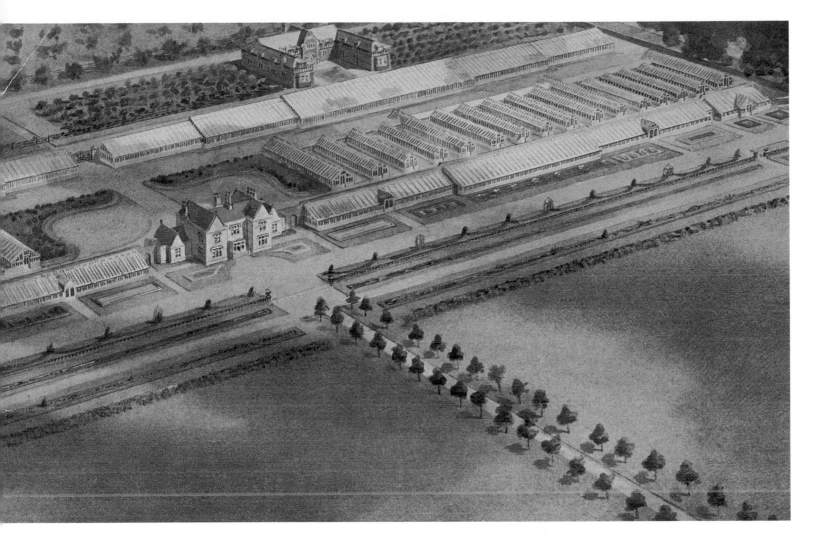

The inquiry report of 1838, pointing to inefficiency and waste, made depressing reading. The result was to be a radical restructuring of the administration and working methods of the royal gardens. This included a recommendation to create a large new kitchen garden at Frogmore, replacing the previous several. Within a few years the kitchen garden was to become a pattern of efficiency in supplying the royal household – virtually wherever it happened to be – with fresh fruit, vegetables and flowers.

It is unclear who designed the new kitchen garden, whose monumental twelve-foot walls are virtually all that remain today. Initially it covered a twenty-seven-acre site at Frogmore to the south of Queen Charlotte's house. Work began in 1841 on what by 1843 was already described as 'the most perfect garden in Europe of its kind'. The hot-houses were 840 feet long and faced south, looking towards thirteen acres of fruit and vegetables. Behind the hot-houses stretched a further four acres with pits, forcing houses, frames and store-rooms, offices and fruit houses. The gardener's house even had two rooms in

AN ILLUSTRATION OF THE GLASSHOUSES, AS THEY WERE RECONSTRUCTED under Edward VII, gives a rare glimpse of the vast fifty-acre kitchen gardens at Windsor. No good visual record of these gardens under Queen Victoria exists but they were laid out on the same lines. The foreground of the illustration omits details of the realities which were walled enclosures filled with vegetables and six miles of trained fruit trees. A carriage drive, flanked by flowerbeds and bell-shaped wire trellises covered in climbing roses, divides the kitchen gardens from glasshouses. The huge range included fourteen vineries (where strawberries and French beans among other plants were also grown), eight peach houses, four melon houses, three fig houses, two tomato houses, six orchid houses, two palm houses, three azalea houses and a fernery. 44,000 cubic feet of teakwood and 156,000 square feet of glass were used in their construction. The other buildings housed offices, store rooms, and living quarters for the gardeners.

which to receive the Queen and the Prince Consort and their guests when they toured the garden. There were flower borders and the vegetables stood in line 'like soldiers on parade'. By 1859 the area had expanded to thirty-four acres, with a man to an acre, and by 1897 to fifty acres. In that year the produce included 5000 lb of grapes, 2000 lb of strawberries (a state ball consumed 70–90 lb), 450 bushels of apples, 1550 lb of gooseberries and 1220 lb of cherries (Victoria's favourite fruit). Figures for the previous year show that it had also supplied 3304 boxes of cut flowers as well as flowers for wreaths, crosses, bouquets and buttonholes. All this reflects the emphasis on reform and good housekeeping which was one of the keynotes of the age.

That reforming zeal was epitomized not by the prodigal young Victoria but by her husband Albert, who quickly became the central figure in Victoria's life. The younger son of the Duke of Sachsen-Coburg-Saalfeld, a tiny principality on the borders of Saxony and Bavaria, Albert as a young man was strikingly handsome, tall and slim with curly brown hair, side whiskers and a moustache. His uncle, King Leopold of the Belgians, the brother of the widowed Duchess of Kent and thus also uncle to Victoria, had cast him in the role of Victoria's future husband early on and as a result much attention had been paid to his education, with extensive travels in Germany and Italy in addition to a spell at the University of Bonn. He was to appear to the average Briton as the German of caricature: high-minded but humourless, applying a deadly seriousness to everything including games and sport, concerned with an unnecessarily pedantic attention to detail and a slavish believer in method. But Albert was a visionary, at home in the world of abstract ideas, and he found himself in a country with an essentially pragmatic attitude and a deep distrust of philosophies. He had a passionate desire to raise the level of public taste, which would be shown in his involvement in the redecoration of the Houses of Parliament and above all in the Great Exhibition of 1851, celebrating the great technological achievements of the age.

Although Victoria was well informed, with a lively and determined mind and a talent for drawing, she had neither Albert's education and application nor his sense of mission. His ideas were inevitably far more progressive than hers and, loving him deeply as she did, her taste became moulded to his. In 1843,

THE PAVILION IN THE GROUNDS OF BUCKINGHAM PALACE, SEEN ACROSS THE lake in 1846 (*above*), was already in existence in 1837 but became a vehicle for the Prince's arts patronage in 1844. He added a balustraded terrace outside, while the inside he had decorated with experiments in fresco painting as a preliminary trial for the redecoration of the Houses of Parliament. Recorded in chromolithographs by Ludwig Grüner, the central octagonal room (*below*) was adorned with a series of panels by leading painters of the day depicting scenes from Milton's masque *Comus*. Sadly, the pavilion was demolished in 1928.

three years after their marriage, Albert's private secretary wrote, 'The Prince is systematically going over the Queen's education and reforming her mind.'

The young couple's happy domestic life would gradually re-establish the monarchy as an institution worthy of public respect. Under Albert's influence, they shunned society of the kind that had been cultivated by George IV and set an example of a life of privilege earned, one based on hard work, simple family pleasures, the following of Christian virtues and a belief that the role of art was to ennoble humankind. Victoria and Albert's gardens are mirrors of these attitudes, which would eventually change the public perception of the royal family in a way which has affected it ever since.

Queen Victoria inherited Buckingham Palace when it was still being built and its gardens were still in the process of being laid out by Aiton. It is striking that no great alterations were made by her to its lay-out and it was only at the close of the 1840s, when Edward Blore had completed the new east wing, that attention was turned to the area now occupied by the Victoria Memorial. William Andrews Nesfield, the apostle of the grand formal Italian manner, produced a magnificent plan with par-terres incorporating the royal monograms and fountains pre-sided over by St George attended by the River Thames, Fame and Victory. This scheme was never carried out and Victoria and Albert's solitary contribution to Buckingham Palace was the interior decoration of an existing garden structure, which became known as the Comus Pavilion.

In this they were assisted by Ludwig Grüner, who was also to act as Albert's amanuensis at Osborne House. Grüner had been trained as a scene-painter and engraver in Dresden before travelling to Spain and France, and then in 1836 to Rome, where he executed a series of engravings of famous Renaissance works of art. He had come to England in 1841 and became the Prince's adviser on art, supervising the interior decoration of the state apartments at Buckingham Palace and also Albert's purchases of Italian and German art.

Grüner's handsome volume with superb chromolithographs entitled *Decorations of the Garden-Pavilion in the Grounds of Buckingham Palace* (1846), recorded the work on the Comus Pavilion. The building itself, demolished in this century, was probably by Wyatville and stood on one of the banks created by Aiton for George IV. Outside, Albert designed a balustraded terrace (an anticipation of Osborne), while within, the rooms were given

THE ROYAL FAMILY POSED OUTSIDE ONE OF THE CONSERVATORIES AT Buckingham Palace in 1854 for the celebrated photographer Roger Fenton. Whenever possible the Queen walked in the gardens here each day, while Prince Albert used the grounds to give natural history lessons to his children.

THE OSBORNE ESTATE IN THE ISLE of Wight was purchased in 1844. The house was begun in 1845 in tandem with the laying out of the grounds. Both were minutely supervised by the Prince Consort, in the case of the house with the architect, Thomas Cubitt, and in that of the garden, Ludwig Grüner, his art adviser. The intent was to create a villa looking back to the Italian Renaissance, with elaborate terraces, balustrading, statuary and fountains, but with flowerbeds in the latest manner and a vast planting of trees to frame both the house and the view to the sea.

THE CONSTRUCTION OF THE terraces was an engineering triumph calling for a cement wall 25 feet high with 11 feet below ground-level. At its base it was 7 feet wide and at the top 2 feet 6 inches. This view of 1847 by W. Leitch (*below*) records the massive earthworks in progress.

over to fresco paintings, which were to act as a practical example of what could be achieved in the new Houses of Parliament. The previous buildings had been largely burnt down in 1834 and their rebuilding by Sir Charles Barry had become an opportunity for heroic decoration by British painters, a project to which the Prince devoted considerable energy. The central octagon of the Pavilion was dedicated to scenes from Milton's masque *Comus*, with works by such leading artists as Dyce, Eastlake and Maclise, while one of the two flanking rooms was decorated in the Pompeian manner and the other with episodes from the novels of Sir Walter Scott.

This was the age of eclecticism, of choice of styles, in a ferment of reaction against what was seen as the dull uniformity of Georgian England. The eclectic styles of the Comus Pavilion were to be reflected on a much greater scale at Osborne and Balmoral, with the first expressing a passion for the Italy of the High Renaissance and the second evoking a mix of Sir Walter Scott's historical romances and the castles of the German Middle Ages. Both were quintessentially Albert's visions, with Victoria as a fervently admiring onlooker.

Osborne arose out of the desire of the young couple, both still in their twenties, to have a real home of their own, something which they discussed on one of their daily walks in the grounds of Buckingham Palace on 19 October 1843. George IV's Pavilion at Brighton was ruled out as a possibility. The town had expanded so much that there were no longer views to the sea and no privacy of any kind, besides which Victoria considered it 'a strange, odd, Chinese-looking thing'. The Queen remembered two childhood summers when her mother had rented Norris Castle on the Isle of Wight, which now in the railway age was only four hours from London. The island promised the seclusion the couple were seeking and when Osborne House came up for sale they made an immediate decision, in October 1844, to purchase it. Both of them had fallen in love with the place.

The three-storeyed Georgian house was inadequate for the couple's rapidly growing family and would need replacing, but

W. LEITCH'S WATERCOLOUR OF the Lower Terrace at Osborne in 1851 (*left*) captures the density of built structure in the garden. Much of the sculpture was mass-produced and chosen from commercial catalogues. The two Medici Lions, cast from those that Albert had seen in Florence, were made in a form of artificial stone by the English firm of Austin & Seely.

THE GARDEN AT OSBORNE WAS, for children, both a source of delights and a school for instruction in the moral virtues. This focussed on the Swiss Cottage (*above*) where the children learned to cook and to garden. A view of 1855 by W. Leitch (*right*) shows the rectangular plots assigned to each child where they grew flowers, fruit and vegetables which they had to sell to their father as a lesson in basic economics. The plots have today been replaced with handsome herbaceous borders (*opposite above*).

both Victoria and Albert were entranced by the splendid setting. Lawns swept dramatically down to the sea, affording wonderful views across the Solent to the mainland downs beyond, and recalled for Albert the Bay of Naples – a resemblance that was to help determine the Italian Renaissance style of both garden and house. By December 1847 the couple would also acquire the other farms and land around, amounting in all to 1727 acres and providing Albert with an opportunity to create not only a garden but an entire landscape.

The Prince, who was to describe his role as 'partly forester, partly builder, partly farmer and partly gardener', supervised every detail of the work which ensued on both the house and garden. To assist him in the realization of his vision, he had Ludwig Grüner for artistic advice and found the architect he needed in Thomas Cubitt. Albert was familiar with Cubitt's work through the house he had built for the Prince's secretary, Charles Anson, but Cubitt was also part of Albert's preferred milieu, for he was very much a man of the new professional classes. An enterprising developer who built large tracts of London, from Bloomsbury to Pimlico, Cubitt had the backing of a highly efficient office whose ability to deliver can be measured by the speed with which the new house was built. The foundation stone of the Pavilion, the couple's own private apartments, was laid on 23 June 1845 and on 14 September 1846 the couple slept their first night there.

Work on the garden had gone ahead simultaneously and in June 1845 Albert was described by Victoria as 'building, demolishing, gardening and measuring'. From the outset the house and its formal environs were to be set into a landscape of Albert's devising, one in which vast plantings of trees were to frame the views to the Solent and, looking backwards, the house itself. 'After luncheon,' the Queen wrote in December 1845, 'we were out for nearly two hours, I helping Albert with his planting which I found very entertaining.' In July 1846 Albert began work on the Pavilion Terrace, an impressive construction calling for huge retaining walls to bear the balustrading and urns. Within it was a formal geometric garden with stone-edged beds and walks laid with imitation lava, a composition recently manufactured by Orsini and Armani in different colours. By the summer of the following year flowerbeds were crammed with geraniums, fragrant stocks and heliotrope. Four statues of the Seasons, which Albert gave to Victoria as a birthday present, and the huge central tazza were added later.

This Italianate garden with its elaborate terracing, balustrading, statues, fountains and parterres, was in the tradition of Thomas Hope's Deepdene, which Loudon in his *Encyclopaedia of Cottage, Farm and Villa Architecture* (1833) had hailed as 'the finest example in England of an Italian villa united with the grounds by architectural appendages'. A steady stream of Italianate gardens had followed, of which the one most likely to have directly influenced Victoria and Albert was Trentham Park, laid out by Sir Charles Barry for the Duke and Duchess of Sutherland

IN HER WATERCOLOUR OF 1850, QUEEN VICTORIA CATCHES THE CULT OF fresh air and atmosphere of family holidays at Osborne (*below*). Depicted, from left to right, are her children who would become Alice, Grand Duchess of Hesse, Alfred, Duke of Saxe-Coburg-Gotha, Edward VII, Helena, Princess of Schleswig-Holstein, Victoria, Empress of Germany, Louise, Duchess of Argyll and, in his nursemaid's arms, Arthur, Duke of Connaught.

THIS FOUNTAIN IN THE CENTRE OF the round basin below the Lower Terrace at Osborne (*right*) is in bronzed zinc. The classical figure of a Boy with a Swan, could be chosen from a catalogue (*below*) and ordered from the Berlin manufactory of Moritz Geiss.

A VIEW LOOKING DOWN ON TO the Lower Terrace today (*right*) sums up the overwhelmingly Italianate nature of Osborne which still deliberately retains its quintessentially Victorian planting schemes. It also shows the large quantities of sculpture, both specially commissioned and mass-produced, which were purchased to adorn the garden. At the centre of the fountain is a bronze figure of Andromeda by John Bell cast by the Coalbrookdale Co. and purchased at the Great Exhibition of 1851. Around it are eight 'marine monsters' from the sculptor William Theed.

between 1834 and 1842. To Victoria, the Duchess of Sutherland could do no wrong in matters of taste and Barry would indeed have been the much more obvious choice of architect for Osborne if Albert had not considered him difficult to work with. Whether or not Victoria and Albert had actually seen Trentham, they certainly knew about this immediate precursor to Osborne with its similarly asymmetrical Italianate house married to symmetrical Italianate gardens.

Behind Albert's vision were also the gardens at his much loved Rosenau, a small castle outside Coburg in which Albert and his brother had grown up. Victoria and Albert visited Rosenau in the year that they began Osborne and Victoria was characteristically enthusiastic; 'my 2nd home', she declared it. The Italianate terraces, balustrading and fountains at Rosenau doubtless fuelled a desire for something similar at Osborne, although it was to be on a much larger scale, and certain features, such as the Swiss Cottage later built for the children, were to be virtually duplicated.

Following the initial phase of work, when the Pavilion Terrace was created, a major decision was taken to construct two further terraces leading from the main building. This was a hugely expensive project, for which Cubitt had up to 250 men working on site at a time to build ramparts and shift earth.

Here more than anywhere else Albert re-created the Italian architecture of the Renaissance period that he but not Victoria had seen. The sequence from the Upper Terrace to the Lower and thence to the avenue of clipped evergreens is based on Bramante's celebrated courtyard linking the Vatican with the Belvedere in Rome, with its double staircase succeeded by a central single one. To one side of the Upper Terrace another double flight of steps leads down to the Orangery and to a walk flanked with Irish yews. The lay-out of the garden spaces, quartered and with statuary or fountains as focal points, is typically Renaissance and so is the stress on the central axis, which runs from the french window at the centre of the main building right through to the avenue into the landscape beyond.

The Upper Terrace was completed by November 1849, when Victoria wrote that it was 'prettily and tastefully laid out. It gives such a finish to the whole place, and makes it look so much larger.' Albert was laying out the garden on the Lower Terrace in March 1851, but it was not until July two years later that the fountain and the paving were finished. The final result, regardless of all the historical influences, is quintessentially Victorian. Despite the attempts at symmetry the garden, like the building, is true to its period in being resolutely asymmetrical.

OSBORNE WAS CENTRAL TO Queen Victoria's life from the time it was purchased until her death there in 1901, and with her family she spent a total of three to four months there each year. Queen Victoria gave this painting (*right*) by Winterhalter of herself nursing Prince Arthur to Albert on his birthday on 16 August 1850. It records the recently completed Pavilion Terrace at Osborne with its massive central tazza planted with an agave.

A FAMILY GROUP ON THE TERRACE at Osborne (*below*) photographed by Caldesi on 26 May 1857 shows, from left to right, Prince Alfred, the Prince Consort, Princess Helena, Prince Arthur, Princess Alice, Princess Beatrice, Queen Victoria, the Princess Royal, Princess Louise, Prince Leopold and the Prince of Wales. The statue behind is one of many bronzed zinc classical figures bought from the German firm of Moritz Geiss.

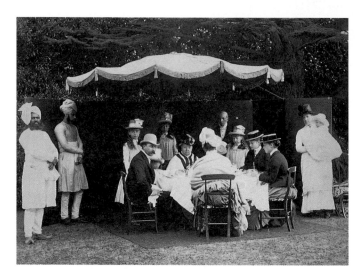

A PHOTOGRAPH OF 1867 SHOWS THE QUEEN AND SOME OF HER FAMILY having tea in the garden at Osborne (above). Throughout her life the Queen spent as much time as possible out of doors. Seen here, from left to right, are two Indian servants, then her granddaughter Princess Marie of Edinburgh, her son Arthur, Duke of Connaught, her granddaughters, Princesses Beatrice and Victoria Melita of Edinburgh, the Queen, her daughter Beatrice, Princess Henry of Battenberg (back view), another servant, her granddaughters Princess Alexandra of Edinburgh and Princesses Alix and Irene of Hesse, and a nurse holding Prince Alexander of Battenberg (Beatrice's eldest child).

UNTIL HIS DEATH, VICTORIA AND ALBERT SPENT BOTH THEIR BIRTHDAYS AT Osborne. On each occasion the presents were arranged in a room bedecked with flowers and swags of myrtle from the garden. So dear to the Queen's heart were these tableaux that she had many, including this one (*opposite*), by James Roberts in 1861, recorded in watercolours.

The planting too was wholly of its era and entirely under Albert's directions. The siting of larger specimens within the broader landscape was often done by means of Albert's signals from one of the towers. In March 1846 Victoria describes how she watched him plant 'a daphne, a magnolia, and two Nerpoles Japonica, very rare and exotic-looking plants'. She herself planted a tulip tree on that occasion. Sometimes very large specimens were obtained, such as bays brought from North-wood Park, which were followed in 1848 by masses of ever-green oaks, Scotch firs and rare Cork oaks, which are still there. In 1854 Albert was busy laying out the principal avenue, which included Cedars of Lebanon, Lucombe and evergreen oaks and he would continue to refine the existing woodland and plant new specimens on the estate over the next six years.

By 1855, however, the planting of the pleasure grounds around the house was virtually completed. In August 1850 the

Magnolia grandiflora, which is still there scenting the summer air, was planted against the wall of the Lower Terrace. The following year the pergola was planted and in April 1853 the Prince was busy putting camellias in the same garden area.

The bedding plants, which fill the flowerbeds with colour in summer, were also the height of fashion by the 1850s, a fashion which had been pioneered by the Duke of Bedford's gardener at Bedford Lodge, Kensington, in the 1830s. The old herbaceous plants had given way to brightly coloured annuals, recent introductions from warmer climes, which could be reared in great quantities in commercial glasshouses and planted out for the summer months in time for the owners' arrival from London at the close of the season. Such a system suited Victoria and Albert, whose main period of residence was during the summer months, and 60,000 bedding plants a year were raised in the greenhouses at Osborne not only for the flower gardens of the

main house but for a whole series of lodges and cottages dotted about the estate. The beds of pelargoniums, lobelias, salvias, plumbago, cannas and calceolarias would have been electrifying in their luminosity, particularly against the strong ochre metallic lava paths, and would have had all the drama of a totally new garden experience. The effect of such hectic tonality might well not be to modern taste but the High Victorian age adored pure colour, as is more appreciated today in works by the Pre-Raphaelite painters.

Victoria and Albert came to Osborne four times a year – in March and April, in May for the Queen's birthday, for a long period from mid-July until well into August and again just before Christmas – but the bedding-out system covered only the late spring and summer visits. The garden in winter could be a desolate sight, as one of the children's tutors, Sir Howard Elphinstone, pointed out in December 1859: 'Those pretty vases, which one cannot help associating with geraniums and other bright-coloured gems, are standing in their damp nakedness almost an eyesore, on the moist terrace.'

Much thought was, however, given to extending the flowering season to cover most months of the year. Early spring had its harbingers. In February 1861 the Queen wrote to her eldest daughter: 'It was a very fine day – very hot sun – everything so green – the trees nearly out – profusion of primroses and violets, kingcups – anemones – oxlips, etc.' And in her journals Victoria responds with delight to the flowering year as it unfolded. She adored spring flowers, above all lily of the valley, and the Prince's substantial plantings of camellias, rhododendrons, azaleas and lilacs, then new and exotic, presented her with 'a lovely sweet nosegay'. In mid-July she was overcome by the fragrance of the honeysuckle, roses, jasmine and the *Magnolia grandiflora*, which lasted well into August.

Her journal captures the family's alfresco existence at Osborne and her genuine delight in the garden. She had a deep belief in the value of fresh air and until the end of her life would spend most of the day in the garden when the weather was favourable. On 18 July 1854 she wrote: 'We breakfasted on the terrace, with its fountains playing and the air perfumed with the smell of orange blossoms, and roses, which quite cover the pergola.' Again a year later on 16 August 1855: 'Sat out under the trees, where it was really heavenly, and sketched. Every day, every year, this dear sweet spot seems more lovely and with its brilliant sunshine, deep blue sea and dazzling flowers, is a perfect paradise – and all my beloved one's creation – the result of his exquisite taste.'

One aspect of that exquisite taste were the lavish quantities of statues, busts, fountains and urns that were part of the garden picture and went in tandem with the interior decoration of the house, which had corridors designed to accommodate a growing collection of contemporary sculpture. For most of the previous century garden ornaments and sculpture had had some sort of iconographic significance, adding to the garden's inner meaning, but by the middle of the nineteenth century they were taking on the purely scenographic role which they occupy today. The use of such artefacts at Osborne shows this turning point, for they are there chiefly as hard-surface accents. They also reflect Albert's great interest in any form of technological advance combined with his desire to evoke Italy.

Many of the items came from the Berlin manufactory of Moritz Geiss, who during the 1840s had perfected a method of bronzing zinc. Among the work Albert bought from Geiss was a group of life-size casts, including the Venus de' Medici and Meleager with his spear, whose handsome effect is rather lost today because of the erosion of the bronze patina. From another foreign company, the Parisian foundry of Miroy Frères, were acquired the four zinc figures of the Seasons. Other pieces in artificial limestone, a cement substance varying in colour from muted grey-white to light brown-yellow, came from the English firm of Austin & Seely. An illustrated catalogue of their wares dated 1844 includes several items at Osborne, among them, apart from urns, two famous classical figures, the Dog of Alcibiades and the famous wild boar, *Il porcellino*, cast from the original in the Uffizi Gallery in Florence.

Not everything, however, was selected from a catalogue. There were specially commissioned items. On the steps leading up from the Andromeda fountain there were eight 'marine monsters', hippocamps with putti astride them, cast in 1858–60, by William Theed, a sculptor greatly favoured by both the Queen and the Prince Consort. The other commissioned piece, from John Francis, was the statue of Albert's beloved greyhound, Eros, who had died on 31 July 1844. One cast is on the Pavilion Terrace, while another marks the dog's grave at Windsor. Visiting Francis' studio to inspect progress the Queen wrote: 'Albert directs everything, and also works himself at it.'

Albert's supervision of everything extended to inculcating gardening as an aspect of moral virtue in his children. Each child was assigned a small plot about half a mile from the house and provided with gardening clothes, including clogs, diminutive tools and wheelbarrows, many of which are still preserved at Osborne. The identical plots consisted of two rows of flowers, gooseberries, strawberries and raspberries, followed by one row each of turnips, onions, beet, carrots, asparagus, peas, beans, parsnips and artichokes. In 1853–54 Albert also had the Swiss Cottage built for his children, a wooden chalet inspired by the one in the grounds of Rosenau and assembled from ready-made sections. Here the royal children learned lessons of domestic economy and also assembled a museum along the lines of their father's 'Kabinet' at Rosenau.

Victoria followed every step of her husband's creation of their paradise by the sea, the precise details of which were to be published in 1880 under the title *A Summary of the Various Works Proposed and Executed on the Osborne Estate From 1845 to 1861 inclusive, By Direction of H.R.H. The Prince Consort*. Her delight, however, was as a receiver, not an originator. She viewed the gardens primarily as an emanation of the man she loved and when, on 14 December 1861, Albert expired in his wife's arms, Osborne assumed the role of a sacred monument to he who had gone.

For the remaining forty years of Victoria's life nothing was to change. The trees and shrubs continued, of course, to grow, which presented Victoria with a problem. 'I did not attend to many things when out with him,' she lamented in retrospect, 'which would be so useful to me now – about trees and planting and plans of his.' The Land Steward, Andrew Toward, had however worked with Albert for over twenty years and he assumed the position of a precious link with the intentions of her late husband. As a result today, even with the simplification resulting from two world wars and economic stringency, both the gardens and the landscape around the house are very much as the Prince Consort laid them out.

It is a garden that continued and developed the return to

THE WEST GARDEN AT BALMORAL,
beneath the private
apartments, was originally a
small geometric parterre whose
focal point was the eagle
fountain given to Queen
Victoria by the King of Prussia.
Today (*above*) it is a rose
garden, chiefly of pink 'Betty
Prior' roses.

FURTHER AWAY FROM THE HOUSE
is a bold herbaceous border
(*left*) at its best during the
present Queen's residence at
Balmoral in August.

OVERLEAF: THE SOUTH FAÇADE OF
Balmoral Castle seen from the
garden planted in the 1920s.

formality shown in George IV's East Terrace Garden of the 1820s at Windsor and, also like George IV's garden, its design paralleled the revivalism in architecture. But whereas at Windsor a geometric garden of an earlier age matched the medieval gothick asymmetry of Wyatville's castle, by the 1840s at Osborne a villa in the Italian style called for an Italianate garden. Osborne, however, is not a great garden when compared with Barry's two masterpieces in that style, Trentham and Shrubland Park, for Prince Albert, whatever his talents, was no Barry. None the less, Osborne set the official seal of approval on the style and as Victoria summed it up in a letter to her eldest daughter in July 1858: 'Osborne is really too lovely . . . the perfume of orange-blossom, magnolias, honeysuckles – roses, etc. of all descriptions on the terrace, the quiet retirement, all make it a perfect paradise – which I always deeply grieve to leave.'

But leave they did every year, heading north for Scotland and Balmoral, which like Osborne was to become a shrine to Albert after 1861. Victoria's first visit to Scotland had been in the summer of 1842, when her and Albert's preoccupation was to

re-establish loyalty to the Crown. Both of them were, however, immediately capitvated by its people and its landscape. To Albert it looked just like Coburg, 'very German-looking', and Loch Tay was declared 'very like Thuringen'. The couple returned again in 1844 and 1847, and Victoria's journals reveal a response to it coloured by travel writers in the picturesque vein and the novels of Sir Walter Scott.

In 1848 they decided to acquire a Scottish house, which, as in the case of Osborne, was done in a rush. The sudden death of Sir Robert Gordon made available the Balmoral lease and Victoria and Albert took it without even inspecting the property. The Deeside area, however, had been recommended to them as having a microclimate with the lowest rainfall in that area of Scotland. The negotiations to purchase proved protracted and it was not until June 1852 that Balmoral finally became theirs. Three months later the foundation stone of the present castle was laid.

Three years' work had preceded this, for within days of their arrival in 1848 Albert had summoned the architect John Smith

THE VICTORIAN KITCHEN GARDEN at Balmoral has long since vanished. The one today, much nearer the castle, dates from the 1950s. It is the only one of the Queen's gardens which still provides the family with produce as well as flowers.

THE QUEEN AND HER GRANDDAUGHTERS, VICTORIA, PRINCESS LOUIS OF Battenberg, and Irene, Princess Henry of Prussia, are pictured (*below*) in 1893 beside her tea-house in the grounds of Frogmore House, attended by her Indian servant, Chidda, and Francis Clark. The tea-house survives totally unchanged from her day (*opposite*); it consists of two buildings, connected by a narrow covered way, one a kitchen and the other a day room with amenities.

of Aberdeen to discuss improvements to the existing house. Due to the wrangles over the purchase these were never carried out and it was Smith's son, William, who worked with Albert designing the new castle in the autumn of 1852. The site was dictated by the magnificent setting of surrounding hills which, to the north, sloped down to the river Dee. The resulting castle was in a style fit partly for a Scottish laird and partly for a Teutonic knight.

Work did not begin on the grounds until 1855 and was completed four years later. At Osborne Albert created the Italy he remembered. Balmoral he formed as far as he could into a British Rosenau set within his native Thuringia. It was to have none of the gardening significance of Osborne – the climatic conditions alone made horticulture difficult – but Balmoral was first and foremost about landscape, one which, under Albert's wand, was transformed into a forest worthy of a setting for a Grimm fairytale.

Balmoral started with a disadvantage, for the south Deeside road running west from Abergeldie passed close to the castle

and it was not until the passing of the Ballater Turnpike Road Act of 16 July 1856, enabling the road to be moved, that the landscape planting could be fully planned. A model of the grounds was made in sand and on it Albert, assisted by a surveyor, James Beattie, and an artist, James Giles, marked out the new avenues, paths, plantations and banks that are visible today. As at Osborne there were huge tree plantings but here they were of a very different kind: firs and above all white poplars, shipped from Coburg, which were intermingled with magnificent specimen trees.

In 1856, a year after they had taken up residence in the new castle, the Queen was already writing: 'Every year my heart becomes more fixed in this dear Paradise and so much more so now that all has become my dearest Albert's own creation, own work, own building, own lay-out, as at Osborne: and his great taste and the impress of his dear hand have been stamped everywhere.'

The amount of garden proper was, however, modest, hardly more than a few enclosures nestling beneath the granite walls of the castle. These gardens were designed by John Thomas, a prolific self-taught sculptor who had worked on Barry's Houses of Parliament and where it is likely that he met the Prince. Sculpture poured from him and he worked for Victoria and Albert at Buckingham Palace and Windsor as well as Balmoral. Here, amongst other things, he carved the bas-reliefs on the west façade of the castle where the main garden was situated. Some of his coloured designs with alternatives for both the west and south gardens still survive, one being annotated 'Approved, Albert'.

The west garden beneath the private royal apartments was the only garden of any importance and even that was small. Victoria records: 'We walked along the river and outside the house . . . the little garden on the west side, with the eagle fountain which the King of Prussia gave me, and which used to be in the greenhouse at Windsor, is extremely pretty; as are also the flowerbeds under the walls of the side which faces the Dee.' The west garden as Victoria knew it has largely gone today. It used to jut out in a large semicircle around which it was possible to wander and enjoy the views. The eagle fountain is also no more, having been disposed of during the First World War.

In Victoria's time the garden was in two parts and the furthest oval section was described in 1876 as having two circular beds cut into the lawn which were thickly planted with roses and edged with violas. Close to the house the garden was rectangular, with the circular eagle fountain at its centre, and flanked by two granite blocks 'with two full-sized bronze deer placed on them'. The garden otherwise was a simple parterre and in 1876 there were two circular beds filled with juniper and with bronze boars at the centre of each. One of these survives, re-sited, and is another version of the *porcellino* at Osborne.

From here a granite stairway gave access to a north-facing flower garden that in 1876 was planted with roses, ericas and

bedding-out annuals, with a fine line of Irish yew. Twenty years later a second account describes the beds filled with flowers such as penstemons, asters, antirrhinums, stocks and clarkia. At the front of the castle, which faced south, there was a series of 'mosaic beds of coloured stones', long since gone, which are a reminder that the Victorian age revived the coloured gravel parterres of the seventeenth century. The east garden was equally modest: a boxwork parterre filled in summer with brilliant annuals around an ironwork fountain.

But Balmoral was about landscape not gardening and after 1861 the evidence of the Queen's grief was to spread over the surrounding countryside. The vast cairn – a traditional Scottish form of landmark or memorial in the form of a pyramid of stones – for Albert still dominates the skyline and was the herald of the long series of commemorative artefacts which Victoria was to dot across the garden and landscape. Further cairns arose to mark marriages such as that of the Prince of Wales to Alexandra of Denmark in 1863 and of her youngest daughter, Beatrice, to Henry of Battenburg in 1885. Statues were

erected in memory of the Prince Consort and Sir Thomas Biddulph, her Keeper of the Privy Purse, and, more contentiously, her devoted Scottish retainer, John Brown. (One of Edward VII's first acts was to remove the statue to a remote part of the estate.) Other children were commemorated by seats or crosses.

Osborne was less burdened with memorials, although sprigs of myrtle from the bouquets of successive royal brides were planted and the grounds had their fair share of memorial trees. Nothing, however, could eclipse Frogmore when it came to transforming a garden landscape (once Queen Charlotte's) into a horticultural version of the *Almanach de Gotha*. An article on Frogmore in 1901 lists over twenty commemorative trees each planted by a member of the vast European royal family to whom Victoria was grandmother. There were also stone memorials, such as crosses and a drinking fountain, to relatives, retainers and friends. All are overshadowed now by Victoria and Albert's mausoleum.

The mausoleum was inspired by the famous Hawksmoor one at Castle Howard, which Victoria had noted as 'very pretty . . .

not at all dreary . . . It is just the sort of thing I wish one day to builld for ourselves.' Its predecessor was that designed by Grüner and A. J. Humbert for the Queen's mother, the Duchess of Kent, which was 'constructed', so the Prince wrote in 1859, 'to be capable of being used as a summer house in the garden'. Victoria and Albert's own mausoleum was the work of the same team but this time working in the Romanesque style with elements inspired by Albert's family mausoleum in the Hofgarten at Coburg. It could never be mistaken for a summerhouse and its haunting melancholic presence means that to most people Frogmore is neither a house nor a garden but a royal graveyard.

For Victoria, however, it was a place of solace where she could gain the peace and solitude she desired. Not only did Frogmore become a shrine to Albert, a place of pilgrimage, but as it was only a short carriage drive away from Windsor Castle – where there was nowhere private to sit out of doors – she used it a great deal. Her obsession with fresh air continued to the end of her life and she spent as much time as possible outside, having breakfast, tea and working under the trees or a special canopy. She had a delightful rustic tea-house built just south-east of the main house, so that she could spend whole days close to her beloved's remains.

The Frogmore that Queen Charlotte had known gradually became more and more overgrown as Queen Victoria walled herself in with evergreen screens of yew, laurel and rhododendrons. Nothing was cut back for, as the article of 1901 ends, 'she does not like any changes'. This was true of all her gardens, which became redolent of the tragedy which overcame her. After the death of Prince Albert, monarchical gardening stood still for forty years.

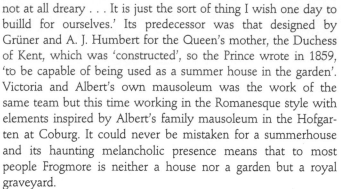

VICTORIA AND ALBERT'S MAUSOLEUM AT FROGMORE, GLIMPSED HERE FROM across the canal (*right*), was inspired by the ones at Coburg and Castle Howard. In the early years of their marriage, the Queen and the Prince Consort had decided to be buried together in their own mausoleum, away from their royal ancestors at St George's Chapel, Windsor. When the Prince died in December 1861, the Queen naturally turned to the architect A. J. Humbert and Grüner, whom Albert had commissioned to build and decorate the mausoleum for the Queen's mother who had died earlier in 1861. The exterior was of stone and granite from different parts of Britain, the interior, designed to reflect the Prince's profound admiration for the work of Raphael, of marbles presented by the sovereigns of Europe. The watercolour by Croft (*left*) of 1861 records Grüner's design. The mausoleum was built so quickly that it was ready to receive the Prince's remains exactly a year after his death. Baron Carlo Marochetti modelled the two recumbent effigies (*above left*) at the same time so that, although the Queen's body only joined that of her husband on her death in 1901, her image here is of a young widow.

ABUNDANCE AND SILENCE

QUEEN ALEXANDRA, WIFE OF EDWARD VII

While Victoria mourned Albert in isolation, a new era was already under way centring on her son, Albert Edward, Prince of Wales (1841–1910), who for forty years was to lead society, playing the part his mother had abdicated. In 1901 he finally succeeded as Edward VII, ushering in the golden decade we know as the Edwardian age which effectively ended not with his death in 1910 but with the outbreak of the First World War in 1914. It was not however the pleasure-loving, gregarious Edward who showed a passionate interest in gardening but his wife, the Danish princess, Alexandra (1844–1925). The daughter of King Christian IX, she married the Prince of Wales in 1863 and throughout her long life would retain the beauty and grace she had as a young woman, with her oval face, flawless complexion and huge aquamarine eyes. Her passion was flowers, a passion that intensified with her increasing deafness, and she created at the couple's home at Sandringham in Norfolk a world of flowers into which she could withdraw and find solace.

The acquisition of a country house for the Prince of Wales had been set

QUEEN ALEXANDRA IN 1902; A DETAIL FROM A PAINTING BY FREDERICK Morgan and Thomas Blinks. Isolated by increasing deafness, she found consolation in the company of animals and in her passion for flowers.

SANDRINGHAM HOUSE, NORFOLK, WAS BUILT DURING THE LATE 1860s, AND IS seen here across one of the new lakes created for it by William Broderick Thomas. In their heyday the gardens reflected all that was new, especially the commitment to wild and woodland plantings, and the cultivation of vast quantities of produce from the kitchen gardens.

in train by Prince Albert in 1861 to coincide with his son's coming of age the following year. By then Edward was already beginning to pursue the interests for which he would all his life show unflagging zeal: beautiful women, shooting, horse racing and, in general, every pleasurable diversion that society could offer. His alarmed parents were anxious that the house be in a remote area of the country away from what they regarded as the corrupting influences of the metropolis – although, in the age of the railway and later of the motor car, those were to prove easily transportable. Albert's death at the end of 1861 did not impede the search and on 4 February 1862 the Prince of Wales went to see Sandringham. Although the eighteenth-

in Edward's pleasure-loving life and, following the etiquette of the age, she acquiesced in a long series of royal mistresses. The couple were nevertheless on affectionate terms and had in common a lack of concern for things of the intellect. Neither of them had ever acquired the habit of reading, which in Alexandra's case may well have intensified her interest in the garden at Sandringham. The Prince of Wales had been brought up to garden at Osborne and he is said to have remarked that had he not been King, he would have liked to have been a gardener. But there is little in his character or lifestyle to suggest that the pursuit of horticulture was dear to his heart.

Sandringham, however, was regarded by both Edward and

A PHOTOGRAPH OF SANDRINGHAM in 1864 (*left*) shows the eighteenth-century house before it was rebuilt, with the original lake and overgrown trees very close to the building. A photograph of *c.* 1910 (*right*) records the main south-west garden façade of the new Sandringham. Where the old lake once stood there stretched, from left to right, a series of three formal gardens: the flower garden, the Italian garden and the pansy garden. These led directly on to the lawns and thence to the woodland and lakes, reflecting the reaction of the period against built terracing, balustrading and statuary.

century house was considered ugly, it was set amidst charming grounds and a few days later the Queen agreed to purchase it.

Sandringham was never meant to be a palace, but the private country retreat of the heir to the throne, where he could go when not at his London residence, Marlborough House. It was acquired in time for his marriage to Alexandra in March of 1863, which initially at least was a love-match. As well as possessing the beauty which Edward prized, Alexandra had a childlike simplicity and ease of manner which endeared her to everyone. She was also very tactful, an attribute which would stand her in good stead both with her mother-in-law and in her marriage. She remained fond of her generous, kind and self-indulgent husband but her unworldly nature, and the hereditary hearing defect which became progressively worse following her third pregnancy in 1867, meant that she would play less and less part

Alexandra as home. The new house built there between 1867 and 1870 was part of the boom in country house building which marked the years down to 1914. Not only were the houses inherited by the old landed classes being enlarged and made more comfortable but new houses were being built by the *nouveaux riches* of the worlds of trade and commerce, for whom a country house was *de rigueur* if they were to achieve acceptance within established society.

The architect of Sandringham House was A. J. Humbert, who had been recommended to the royal family by Cubitt and who also worked at Osborne and Frogmore. Built in the Jacobean style, it would later have a ballroom added and, after a fire in 1891, a new wing. It was designed for a new phenomenon of the age: the weekend. By the 1890s thirty guests at a time might come for one of the Prince's vast shooting parties, each bringing their personal valet or maid. Together with the members of the royal family and their own domestic, garden and estate staff, the number of people to be accommodated and fed ran into hundreds. The Prince and Princess of Wales were in residence during a great part of the winter months, spending most of November through to the end of February there, including both their birthdays. These were the months punctuated by the Prince's shooting parties, at which the total head of game killed increased over the years from seven to thirty thousand, and they were also therefore the months when the gardens needed to look as good as possible for the visitors.

The gardens at Sandringham were designed by one of the

scheme for Buckingham Palace if it had been executed, began to come under increasing attack. In a strong reaction against High Victorian formality, parterres, numerous garden buildings and sculpture went out of fashion. Horticulture, it was felt, had been swamped by gravel and stonework. A new and powerful garden voice was to be heard, that of William Robinson, whose *Alpine Flowers for English Gardens* (1870) and *The Wild Garden* (1870) appeared at precisely the time when Thomas was engaged at Sandringham. *The Wild Garden*, a plea for the planting of indigenous wild flowers in the garden in a natural state, would have found a ready response in the Princess of Wales, who is recorded as having spent her time trying to stop the gardener

leading landscape gardeners of the late Victorian period, William Broderick Thomas. His nephew, Francis Inigo Thomas, would write of his uncle in 1926 that he 'gave up fox-hunting for laying out the places of country gentlefolk in the prevailing "landscape" manner'. His hunting interests would certainly have recommended him to the Prince, who may have seen his work at Felbrigg Hall, not far from Sandringham at Cromer. Thomas was not an innovative gardener but rather mirrored trends inaugurated by others. In the 1860s he had worked in the Italianate style of William Andrews Nesfield, who made popular the idea of elaborate parterres set within architectural terraces, but by the time he received the Prince of Wales's commission to lay out Sandringham he had changed direction.

During the 1870s the Italianate architectural style, of which Osborne was the great royal exemplar and even more Nesfield's

embarking on grand bedding-out schemes, preferring instead 'my poor innocent inexpensive little flowers'.

Thomas's biggest change to the pleasure grounds was moving the existing ornamental lake which lay close to the house and making two lakes with numerous cascades and rivulets further away. While making the garden he broke his leg and Alexandra's kindness to him was such that afterwards he always sent her flowers on her birthday. Under the Princess's influence, the garden was quite unlike any Thomas had previously designed. There was no built terracing around the house. Instead, a grassy bank led from the main west-facing façade of the house to formal parterres cut into the lawn, which continued in a sweep until it met the encompassing swaths of woodland. The planning, however, is typically late Victorian. The parterres face south-west and are sited so that they could be seen from the drawing room. Today the only evidence of what once formed a series of formal gardens along this side of the house are two well-heads which once acted as focal points.

One of these gardens was the pansy garden. Pansies were one of Alexandra's favourite flowers, and doubly important because they were winter flowering. They were planted in box-edged beds beside gravel paths and their colour could change from season to season according to what was raised in the glass-houses. The other, so-called Italian, garden was designed, some-what surprisingly, by Queen Victoria's cousin, Mary Adelaide, the Duchess of Teck, mother of the future Queen Mary, and was laid out in 1872. High-spirited and popular, the Duchess was a great friend of both the Prince and Princess of Wales, staying regularly at Sandringham.

In its summer glory the Italian garden was a triumph of the head gardener's art. Each year within its basic structure of gravel paths, grass borders and clipped cones of golden holly and yew, a different configur-ation of annuals would be bedded out in a geometric pattern, using such flowers as fuchsias, pelargoniums and calceolarias framed by ribbons of grey foliage plants. In winter the beds were filled with a variety of small shrubs in shades of green, gold and silver 'which makes them cheerful in the dull season': golden yew and box, Portugal laurel, berberis, aucubas, hollies and euonymus. These were underplanted with thousands of bulbs for the spring. Winter bedding-out in this way, an inven-tion of the 1860s, catered for precisely the period when the Prince and Princess were in residence.

The formality of the flower gardens near the house quickly gave way to more original features of the garden, of which the rockery was perhaps the most significant. The fashion for rock-eries and the new forms of planting which they entailed was at its height during the 1860–70s. In the eighteenth century rock-work had been confined to grottoes or cascades, as at Virginia Water, but by the middle of the nineteenth century huge rocky terrains were constructed, simulating as closely as possible natural rock formations; they incorporated mounts and passage-ways, winding paths and coombs. A number of specialist firms emerged which made artificial rock, one of the earliest and most successful of which was that founded by James Pulham of Broxbourne in Hertfordshire. He evolved a clay-based artificial stone which could be fashioned and fired into boulders of giant size. The rockery overlooking the upper lake at Sandringham

was one of Pulham's most important commissions and set the seal of royal approval on the firm.

Thomas used the Pulhamite stone to create not only the rocky cliffs which overlook the lake but also waterfalls, path-ways and a stream – which still meanders through the grounds. He wrote to James Pulham telling him, 'I am very *much* pleased with your work, and I consider the Boat House [concealed beneath the rocky promontory] quite a work of art.' Their royal highnesses, he was sure, would be delighted with everything.

The rockwork, lake and its environs indeed capture the spirit of Alexandra's Sandringham garden. It was a response to all that was new in the 1870s. There was 'the glade' of elms and Scotch pines underplanted with drifts of daffodils and narcissi; the 'wild garden' (pure Robin-son) with lily of the valley, bluebells, primroses, snow-drops, aconites, mulleins and foxgloves, followed in sum-mer by tumbling masses of sweet briars; 'the dell', an imitation of wild woodland so natural that 'the garden-ers are unable to make this spot appear more wild than Her Majesty would like it to be'.

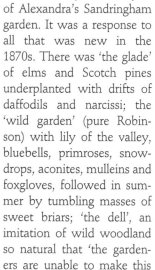

Cyril Ward, writing in 1912 in his *Royal Gardens*, gives us an idea of how effective was all the new planting of the rockery and lake: 'Hundreds of choicest water-lilies float upon its sur-face. Aquatic plants of almost every kind fringe its margin. Clumps of bulrushes, loosestrife, saxifrage, lobelia cardinalis, bamboos and grasses of numberless varieties, have been planted with an artistic negligence which has encouraged nature to help, and has nowhere defied her teaching.'

Plants were the central focus of Alexandra's garden and this reflects a great shift from the previous century. Visitors to the royal gardens of the eighteenth century were taken on a voyage through a landscape of ideas and symbols. Now such a tour was a horticultural feast; skills which before had been banished behind the walls of the kitchen garden or secreted in hidden flower gardens were now on full display so that guests of the royal couple could admire the thousands of new trees, shrubs and flowers that had arrived from the four corners of the earth. The Princess collected in particular the new acers from Japan which brought to the garden a hitherto unknown brilliance of autumn colour.

For this myriad of beautiful new plants to be seen at their best called for intensive labour and it was in the late Victorian period that the head gardener emerged as a person of pro-fessional standing. Sandringham in its heyday in the 1890s was

presided over by Archibald Mackellar, who had been head gardener to the Duke of Roxburghe at Floors Castle. He came south to rule over Sandringham's hundred acres of pleasure grounds, to organize the gardening staff which by the turn of the century numbered over ninety, to see that the kitchen gardens were not only immaculate but productive and that the flower gardens and borders were kept for as long as possible full of bloom. It was his responsibility to plant the formal parterres before the west front each year, for which vast numbers of annuals were raised in readiness for planting in a pattern of his devising. Stretching through the acres around the house there were rare trees and shrubs to tend on the lawns, bulbs to be naturalized in the glades, water plants to care for in the lakes, apart from a plethora of roses, alpines and herbaceous plants.

Under Alexandra, first as Princess of Wales and then as Queen, the gardens continued to multiply, especially the herbaceous borders, which wound their way like garlands through the woodland glades. This expansion seems to have come mainly in the era of Mr MacKellar who, in 1896, designed and planted for Alexandra the royal Rosary on the site of an old tennis court. It contained no less than 1300 dwarf, standard and climbing varieties of roses, supplied by the famous firm of William Paul. Formal in structure, the Rosary was enclosed within wire treillage which was smothered in roses, some of them kitchen gardens and the stables. Photographs show that it was

THE MAGNIFICENT RIBBONS OF EXTRAVAGANTLY PLANTED BORDERS THAT meandered through the woodland glades at Sandringham are captured by Cyril Ward's watercolour of c.1912. (*above*)

ONE OF THE ORIGINAL STONE PLANTERS THAT BRINGS YEAR-ROUND COLOUR to the terrace at Sandringham (*opposite*).

OVERLEAF: THE PLANTING AROUND THE LOWER LAKE AT SANDRINGHAM, dug in the 1860s, has been vastly simplified today, using a scheme chiefly of conifers.

soaring up from containers fastened to the wire walls. Within the garden there was a summerhouse, a fountain around a column with St George and the Dragon on the top of it and a wire rose temple dripping with roses.

A dairy with a Dutch garden in front of it was also created for Alexandra. This catered for the milk provided by a herd of cows imported from her homeland in Denmark. It takes its place in a long line of royal dairies stretching back to Queen Caroline's at Richmond; and like her predecessors, Alexandra used it rather as an elaborate garden pavilion, entertaining or taking tea there. Although some of the Minton tiles and plates which decorated the dairy still survive, both the building and the garden are now no more than a dip in the grass between the abandoned kitchen

THE KITCHEN GARDEN AT SANDRINGHAM, ONE OF THE GREATEST OF THE
Victorian age, became even more splendid in the 1890s when the
Prince of Wales's racing prize-money was lavished upon it.
The great pergola, recorded (*above*) in a watercolour of *c.*1913 by Cyril
Ward, led on to the central path of the main, walled kitchen garden
where the acres of vegetables were concealed from view by
spectacular herbaceous borders backed by apples and roses trained
over arches.
The apple store, photographed in *c.*1907 (*opposite above*) was one of a
series of garden service buildings which were erected in the early
1890s and regarded as models of their sort.
The huge range of glasshouses, rebuilt in 1897 and superbly heated
and equipped to provide the house with a never-ending supply of fruit
and flowers, was linked by corridors, of which this photograph of
*c.*1913 (*opposite below*) gives a glimpse.

The tour of the kitchen garden encompassed the garden's
offices and buildings, which were heated, along with the glasshouses, by the massive boilerhouse. 'Looking down [at this]
from the iron platform', a visitor said, was like 'surveying the
engine room of some great steamer'. An underground reservoir
containing some 15,000 gallons of water was excavated to fulfil
the needs of the glasshouses, and separate stables were built to
house the dray-horses who worked the gardens. Today only the
shells of the office range abutting one of the exterior walls of the
kitchen garden can be seen: the potting-shed, the packing shed,
the painter's workshop and the grape room capable of ripening
between 1500 and 2000 bunches at a time. Next came the seed
store, the mushroom house, then a greenhouse 'filled with
showy flowers', a fruit store-room seventy foot long, and next
to that the bothies, accommodation for the young bachelor

gardeners, which were designed to house twelve men and were regarded as models of their kind.

Sandringham's was an ideal country house kitchen garden and in 1905 it was given a fitting frontispiece with the building of the great pergola whose designer is unknown. Seventy yards long and fifteen yards wide, it was supported by huge brick pillars that bore the massive roof timbers of oak supplied from the estate. A well-head again acts as its focal point but was here flanked by bays with curved marble benches designed by the President of the Royal Academy, Sir Lawrence Alma-Tadema. Over the pergola tumbled roses, honeysuckle, clematis, ceanothus and escallonias, while on either side ten-foot-wide borders were filled with herbs and flowers in shades of blue and white: lavender, stocks, rosemary, sage, hollyhocks, campanulas, lilies and tobacco plants. The structure of the formal flower garden, known as the Square Garden, which stretched towards the gardener's house on the north side, is still basically there today. It gives an indication of a wonderful Edwardian garden with geometrically shaped beds cut into the turf which have, at their centres, metal poles with crowns at the top to support roses. Weeping standard roses acted as vertical focal points to other beds which would have been crammed full of bedding plants.

The Sandringham garden of Alexandra was a reflection of a society in which the appearance of the flower garden, the treasures in the orchid house and the quality of the asparagus served at dinner were all indexes of social prestige. It was an era on which the sun was soon to set. The King died before the world he had known would be totally shattered by the 1914–18 war and its aftermath, but the Queen lived on until 20 November 1925, remaining a lonely figure at her beloved Sandringham. The British royal family remained one of the few European royal families to survive the upheavals but Alexandra was unable to come to terms with the new reality. She had never known the meaning of economy and when her daughter-in-law, Queen Mary, suggested that she reduce the number of flowers in the house, her reaction was that 'It is very difficult as I do like a lot of lovely flowers about the house and in my rooms.'

Perhaps a perfect cameo of this lost age is provided by the Nest, which still stands on a promontory of the rockery overlooking the upper lake. It is a small stone structure decorated on the inside with tiles and adorned with quotations from Tennyson. A dedication here reads: 'The Queen's Nest. A small offering to "The Blessed Lady". From Her Beloved Majesty's Old Servant General Probyn. 1913.' Sir Dighton Probyn served the royal couple for half a century but not even he in his capacity as Comptroller and Treasurer to the widowed Queen could instil in his 'blessed lady' the virtue of thrift. But seated in the Nest gazing out over the lake with its limpid reflections and lilies to the woodland beyond, one feels close to the frail, deaf and almost blind but still beautiful old lady living amidst the ghosts of the Edwardian age. She was to leave it to her successors to come to terms with a social revolution.

PRIVACY AND RETRENCHMENT

GEORGE VI AND QUEEN ELIZABETH

When the glamorous and wayward Edward VIII, later Duke of Windsor, abdicated at the end of 1936, his younger brother, the Duke of York, suddenly found himself inheriting the throne as George VI (1895–1952). A shy and retiring man who found speaking on public occasions an ordeal, he took on the role with considerable misgivings but through his tenacity and sense of duty he scored a tremendous personal triumph. In this he was much aided by Queen Elizabeth, the present Queen Mother (born 1900). He had married Lady Elizabeth Bowes-Lyon, the ninth child of the Earl and Countess of Strathmore, an ancient Scottish family, in 1923, and first as the

GEORGE VI AND QUEEN ELIZABETH, THE QUEEN MOTHER, AS
Duke and Duchess of York; details of portraits by Philip de Laszlò,
painted at the time that they were creating the gardens of Royal Lodge.

THE GARDENS AT ROYAL LODGE AT WINDSOR ARE A SPECTACULAR EXEMPLAR
of the woodlands with flowering shrubs that were so typical of the
years between the wars. They reflected both a need to reduce labour
costs and a desire to create a more relaxed ambience in tune with an
emancipated era. This walk of azaleas leads to a statue of Charity
copied, at the behest of Queen Elizabeth The Queen Mother, from
the original by John Cheere which stands in the gardens at her family
home at St Paul's, Waldenbury.

A GARDEN GATE LEADING TO THE GRAVELLED FORECOURT AT ROYAL LODGE
(*above*) epitomizes the duality of mood of the 1930s, with a lush
romantic planting of climbers – a yellow Banksian rose and a white
wisteria – softening the starkly modernist white walls.

THE REMNANTS OF ROYAL LODGE, GEORGE IV'S NOTORIOUS *COTTAGE ORNÉ*,
were transformed between 1931 and 1939 by the Duke and Duchess
of York into a private family retreat. The house (*right*) is set upon a
handsome terrace designed by Geoffrey Jellicoe which leads down to
sweeping lawns on which stand two great cedars of Lebanon that date
from the time of the Prince Regent.

Duke and Duchess of York and then as King and Queen, they
with their two young daughters, the Princesses Elizabeth and
Margaret, came to embody for the nation a royal domestic idyll
of a kind not seen since Victoria and Albert. Both of them were
also knowledgeable and keen gardeners. The Duchess had
inherited her garden passion from her mother, Lady Strathmore,
who had created a remarkable garden at Glamis Castle. The
Duke gained his on acquiring Royal Lodge, in 1931. And it was
this shared horticultural passion which helped to form a new
image of the Crown after the crisis of the Abdication.

The royal gardens had already been affected by the dramatic
changes in the role of the monarchy since 1918. Even before the
First World War the great royal gardens of the past, Hampton
Court, Kensington, St James's, Brighton Pavilion, Osborne, Rich-
mond and Kew, had passed into the public domain. Windsor
Great Park had been opened to the public, with brass band

concerts being held in the East Terrace Garden in summer. In
1908 Sandringham had opened its gates for the first time,
although Balmoral only followed in the reign of the present
Queen, when Frogmore, too, would become much more accessible. Today, only Buckingham Palace garden remains closed,
although considering the thousands of guests who annually
assail its lawns at the garden parties, it can hardly be categorized
any longer as a mysterious private domain.

These changes reflected the vanishing political power of the
monarchy and the new image of it that was slowly emerging
and being deliberately projected. By their exemplary domestic
life Victoria and Albert had laid the foundations for popular
monarchy, but it was the reign of George V, from 1910 to 1936,
that established the monarchy's dual image of public grandeur
and private probity, upon which it has attempted to rest ever
since. The gardens belong to the private part of the image, the

monarch as country lover, which George VI would be the first to exemplify followed by his daughter and grandson, Elizabeth II and the Prince of Wales.

The monarchy's new role as a symbol uniting an empire and then a commonwealth above class, race or creed was developed through the images presented by mass circulation newspapers and later radio and television. Gardening, for these purposes, was a classless, uncontroversial activity and its earliest use in this way was when a rose garden in Regent's Park was named after Queen Mary. Yet although she had a love of flowers and gardens the Queen's active interest in horticulture could only be described as limited (George V had none); it was expressed in a single garden made at Balmoral. Otherwise Queen Mary is remembered more for demolishing the Comus Pavilion in the grounds of Buckingham Palace and for her 'gang warfare' against ivy at Badminton during the Second World War.

Her son and daughter-in-law, however, were actively interested in gardening and the public image of George VI and Queen Elizabeth's enjoyment of gardens was a reflection of a private reality. Their main gardening creation was at Royal Lodge in Windsor Great Park, which George V had presented to the then Duke and Duchess of York in 1931. This was at the same time as the Civil List was cut, in response to the country's economic depression and the abandonment of the Gold Standard, and as his contribution to the necessary economies the Duke gave up hunting and sold his horses. In the autumn of 1931 he bemoaned their loss in a letter to Ronald Tree, Master of the Pytchley Hunt, who was also a gardening friend. A very rich American, Ronnie Tree, and his wife Nancy were to buy Ditchley in Oxfordshire in 1933 and the work on the house and garden there would have a significant influence on the development of Royal Lodge after 1936.

What the Yorks inherited in 1931, against the backdrop of that year's financial crash, was the remnant of the building left after William IV's demolition, set amidst the landscape George IV had created, although by now it was mostly invisible through a century of tangled undergrowth. Gradually, as the economic crisis lessened, the house was put in order, with new, pink-washed wings added, and work began clearing the land around it, an area of some fifteen or sixteen acres.

The Duke's interest in gardening began, he later said, 'when I had a garden of my own', and he visited other gardens to get

went back to 1875 but it was in the 1920s and 1930s that Lord Aberconway formed his huge collection of rhododendrons there. The Exbury estate had been purchased in 1919 by Lionel de Rothschild who transformed what had been part of the New Forest into a two-hundred-acre woodland garden with a superb rhododendron and azalea collection. In addition, just near to the Yorks, at Fort Belvedere in Windsor Great Park, the Duke's brother, the future Edward VIII, with whom he shared a keen hands-on gardening approach, was also laying out a woodland garden featuring rhododendrons.

THE TERRACE AT ROYAL LODGE (*opposite*) was architecturally the height of 1930s modernism but also catered for the social mores of the period when it was the scene for sunbathing and eating alfresco. These out-of-doors activities called for new types of furniture of the kind pulled along by the Princesses Elizabeth and Margaret Rose (*left*). The trellis-work and mildly Art Deco planters are painted white, the colour made fashionable in the 1930s by the interior decorator Syrie Maugham.

ideas for Royal Lodge. His preference was for informality and the type of garden that he wanted was a woodland garden, on the lines of those pioneered by William Robinson and Gertrude Jekyll, which was considered appropriate for the area beyond the confines of the formal enclosures and lawns around the house. The gardens were made by clearing the existing wood-land, thinning the trees and creating vistas and walks; any fine old trees, some dating from the time of George IV, were pre-served and set off to advantage and the spaces between were embroidered with flowering shrubs, above all rhododendrons and azaleas, and drifts of naturalized bulbs.

In planting a garden like this the Yorks were following a fashion that was enormously popular in the period between the wars. It had the advantage of being not only beautiful but also comparatively cheap to maintain. They certainly knew the two great examples, Bodnant and Exbury. The gardens at Bodnant

The Yorks had help of a practical kind immediately to hand in the person of Eric (later Sir Eric) Savill, who had just formed the Prince of Wales's rhododendron collection at Fort Belvedere in 1930. He became Deputy Surveyor of the Great Park at Windsor in 1931 and in 1937 was appointed Deputy Ranger by George VI, who had become Head Ranger the previous year. Soon after his first appointment, struck by the absence of any garden in the Park, Savill began to turn a small damp area of Englefield Green into a bog garden. From this, under the aegis of Savill, and with the active encouragement of the King and Queen, grew the present thirty acres of the Savill Gardens whose springtime glory remains magnolias, cherries, rhododen-drons and azaleas.

By the time that George VI died in 1952 the woodland garden sprawled over some ninety acres, of which less than a quarter came directly under the supervision of the head gardener at

Royal Lodge, the rest being tended by the staff of the Commissioners of Crown Lands. Over this vast expanse the King had created a magical flower-bespangled woodland landscape, embracing a rhododendron walk, an azalea garden and walk, and a rhododendron species garden. These plantings were punctuated by handsome specimen trees such as a *Davidia involucrata* and *Eucalyptus gunnii*. There were also dazzling magnolias with their scented star-like flowers and the rich tints and glossy dark-green leaves of camellias. It was in essence and remains today a springtime garden designed to be at its best during the months that the family were most in residence, April, May and June.

This woodland garden was well advanced before work began in 1936 on the area immediately surrounding the Lodge. By then the Duke had become an expert on rhododendrons and wrote a delightful letter of gratitude to the Yorks' gardening friend, Violet, Countess of Stair, which called for a botanical as well as a Latin dictionary, for he wrote in 'the language of rhododendrons': 'As to my visit, I am overjoyed Eclecteum [to be chosen out] and Aberrans [wandering] Cyclium [round] so many Erastum [lovely] and Arizelum [notable] gardens in so short a time.'

The new woodland surroundings of Royal Lodge needed to be related to its architecture and immediate gardens, and for this, in 1936, the Yorks called on the services of the young landscape architect, Geoffrey (later Sir Geoffrey) Jellicoe. Jellicoe had studied at the Architectural Association, of which he was later Principal, and had made his mark in 1925 with a book he produced jointly with J.C. Shepherd called *Italian Gardens of the Renaissance*. Its measured drawings showed some of the most famous of these gardens, whose genius 'lay in being sympathetic to the country in which they had planted themselves'. The preoccupation with the Italian garden looked both backwards to the pre-1914 revival of interest, represented by the writings of Sir George Sitwell and Edith Wharton, and forwards in that these gardens' geometric and harmonic qualities seemed to reinforce the principles of the modernist movement to which Jellicoe was committed.

Jellicoe's work reflects the dualism of attitude that haunted most of the arts in Britain, including garden design, after 1918. The response to the past swung between the two poles of rejection and derision, admiration and emulation, while, at the same time, there was all the excitement of modernist ideas, which in their initial phases had none of their later threatening Socialist overtones. Jellicoe's work is full of these contradictions, as much as Cecil Beaton's was in photography or Frederick Ashton's in the ballet. The Yorks knew the work of Jellicoe for Ronnie Tree at Ditchley, a great palladian house by James Gibbs where Jellicoe, in his earliest commission, had built a huge terrace, forming a platform on which to relax in the landscape setting in the new era of sunbathing and the cocktail. He also designed an elaborate formal garden stretching away from another façade of the house; its focus was a long narrow parterre and it was bounded on each side by pleached lime walks,

THE NEW FORMAL GARDEN AT SANDRINGHAM WAS DESIGNED FOR GEORGE VI by Geoffrey Jellicoe just after the Second World War. This view (*right*) is from the King's rooms on the first floor which looked directly down on to the patterns created by the clipped box hedging. The garden was planted where the old driveway had been positioned and, combined with the dense screening beyond, blocked the view from the gates. It also provided areas of privacy within its green 'rooms' for the royal family to sit outside.

WHEN THE LAY-OUT OF SANDRINGHAM IS SEEN FROM THE AIR (*left*), IT becomes clear how the new formal garden – and the evergreen planting just beyond it – secured privacy for the house. The new garden, a rectangle of green, lies to the north-west of the house. The gates can be discerned further towards the top left of the photograph. The old drive used to lead directly from there to the house; it now curves behind the screening evergreens and approaches the front door from the north-east. The large walled kitchen garden and glasshouses stretch out further north-east, and the two lakes fall away from the house towards the south.

the climax to the central vista, a swimming pool, disguised by a curtain of water jets. This garden was clearly inspired by Italy and in particular by the villa Jellicoe admired most, Gamberaia, and it was important in gaining him his first royal commission. Moreover, Jellicoe was also working at this period for the Duchess's brother, David Bowes-Lyon, on a garden which she knew well and loved, St Paul's, Waldenbury.

With Italian villas and Ditchley in mind, Jellicoe provided Royal Lodge with a handsome terrace that runs the length of the rear façade, leading at the north end to a circular enclosure held in by trellis-work with a flight of steps inviting descent on to the lawns. A month before the outbreak of war in 1939 G.C. Taylor and Christopher Hussey wrote enthusiastically in *Country Life* of the transformation of what they regarded as a drear Victorian gothick pile into the acme of thirties modernity. Admiring the 'streamlined' design of the new garden terraces, they described the effect as 'tying the house to its site and emphasizing the sweeping contours in which it is set'. They saw this as 'a clever realization of a contemporary trend in landscape design that seeks to relate modern architecture to traditional English settings' and likened the new Royal Lodge to 'a clean-cut modern building'.

George VI and Queen Elizabeth were seen as being thoroughly up-to-date and in using Jellicoe, a rising lion of a new generation, they also had the input of his partner Russell Page, who after the war had an international practice, creating his greatest gardens outside Britain. At Royal Lodge he contributed to the lay-out and planting of the series of small enclosed gardens surrounding the house, in particular a sunken garden held in by a beech hedge and filled with herbaceous beds.

Jellicoe and Page between them established what we largely still see today: the handsome indented yew hedges which frame the building and form the approach and entrance court, and the gardens immediately either side, in one of which the two young Princesses gardened and in the other of which stood the Wendy House, given by the people of Wales to the Princesses in 1932, with a tiny formal garden before it. Jellicoe's final work was the starkly modernist swimming pool completed in 1938.

In 1953, the year after George VI's death, Jellicoe paid tribute to the King's gardening commitment. 'King George,' he wrote, 'knew precisely what he wanted in landscape.' Instructions were often accompanied by his own pencil notes, and the design was developed from discussion of these. But his involvement went much further than purely paper design. 'He would pass constantly from drawings to the site and back again . . . and he took a hand in all setting-out by the contractor.' As Jellicoe stressed, the conception of the King's gardens was his alone; they were 'a projection of his own personality', and 'he desired no pomp and ceremony'. But the whole garden was a joint enterprise of both the King and Queen, and Jellicoe recalls their enthusiasm in joining in with tape-measures when planning the terrain. The modernist connotation in the garden is a direct corollary to the Queen's commitment to contemporary British art, while her leanings towards romanticism are shown in her love for old-fashioned flowers in profusion, sweet-pea colours and anything fragrant.

Royal Lodge, originally the private garden of a younger son of the monarchy, and modest by the standards of previous royal gardens, was the creation of a few fugitive years before the dislocation of war. The impact of the First World War, when

the gardens of Buckingham Palace had been partly given over to vegetables, was minimal compared to the horticultural devastation of 1939–45. The King and Queen threw themselves with wholehearted commitment into the war effort, part of which was the campaign 'Dig for Victory'. They led the way, putting huge tracts of all the royal gardens to productive use. They also lost most of their labour force when the gardeners were called up for military service and, more significantly, unlike in 1918 they were not to return when peace came. The age of cheap labour, both inside and outside the house, had gone for ever. Even the untaxed financial resources of the royal family were not sufficient to maintain the labour-intensive gardens inherited from the Victorian period. The change is indicated by the fact that there were fifty-eight gardeners at Sandringham in 1939; by 1980 there were only twelve.

George VI and Queen Elizabeth were the first monarchs to be faced with such a situation. Lanning Roper, the American land-scape designer, referred to Sandringham in 1953 and the 'gradual cutting down and simplification demanded by the difficult times in which we live, for the royal gardens are not immune to economic problems'. Although the great herbaceous borders, a fifth of a mile long in the kitchen gardens, were still there, it was 'a major effort to maintain them through the war years with the shortage of labour'. Sandringham, in fact, was the first garden where decisions about retrenchment were made. All the formal gardens on the south-west front were grassed over.

Another change to be faced was that this was the age of the motor car and the splendid Norwich Gates, the main entrance to Sandringham presented to Edward VII by the people of Nor-folk on his marriage, no longer guaranteed privacy, for through both the gates and the flanking railings the house and its sur-roundings were open to view. So, in 1947, Geoffrey Jellicoe was called on to make a new approach road leading to the forecourt and to design a new garden on the north side beneath the King's

AN ELEGANT PLEACHED LIME walk (*left*), one of two which flank the new formal gardens at Sandringham, provides a vista towards the south-west façade of the house which once looked over the Victorian gardens. Jellicoe's classical geometry is strangely at variance with the asymmetrical and exuberant neo-Jacobean style of the architecture.

PINK ROSES AND A CLOUD OF shasta daisies contribute to Sandringham's summer glory (*right*). Although the new formal garden is not as labour-intensive as the pre-war formal gardens – which required replanting almost entirely twice a year – the double rows of pleached limes, immaculately clipped box hedges and lavish herbaceous planting require considerable skill and upkeep.

THE GARDEN AT BIRKHALL IS A LATE VICTORIAN REVIVAL OF A TRADITIONAL Scottish pleasaunce, a decorative yet productive garden with a mixture of flowers, fruit and vegetables. The structure was retained by the Queen Mother but enlivened by her planting preferences, above all the stunning double border of pink *Phlox paniculata* 'Windsor' backed by sweet peas trained on wires which bisects the garden.

THE 250-FOOT BORDER (*above*) WHICH WINDS ROUND THE BELL-SHAPED garden in front of the house at Birkhall is devised to be at its most spectacular in the late summer and autumn when the Queen Mother is in residence there. Perennials such as achillea, rudbekia, solidago, lythrum and sedum are planted in effective blocks, and any spaces filled with annuals such as these ornamental cabbages.

A view looking over the garden (*right*) shows the bright spires of lythrum above the tops of apple trees which are espaliered against the grey stone wall (seen in the photograph *opposite*), while a narrow path lined with white heather and, on one side with red roses, runs along the top of the grass bank that leads down to the rows of vegetables below.

apartments. For the approach he repeated what he had done at Royal Lodge, planting a huge indented yew hedge to enclose a forecourt and frame the house.

The new garden was a long narrow rectangle in the Renaissance compartmented style; box hedges delineated beds and formed 'rooms', and a circle at the centre was intended to have a fountain as its focal point, although this has never materialized. The main vista now culminates with a statue of Time, purchased by Queen Mary in 1950. Elegant pleached lime walks bound the garden on either side and the flowerbeds, originally planted by Dame Sylvia Crowe, were filled with herbaceous plants. The design was essentially a re-run of the formal garden Jellicoe had made at Ditchley. The result at Ditchley, a palladian building inspired by Italian Renaissance villas, was a perfect marriage of house and garden. Sandringham, in sharp contrast, is a rambling Victorian neo-Jacobean pile and although Jellicoe's garden is beautiful, his attempt to marry classical order to Victorian exuberance is at best uneasy.

The garden was still in its infancy when in February 1952 the King died, aged fifty-seven, and it was to remain unfinished. Even during his last illness he was reading and correcting the proofs of a book to be published in 1952 entitled *The Royal Gardeners,* written by one W.E. Shellwell-Cooper who was Principal of the Horticultural Training Centre at Thaxted in Essex. Such a publication, for which the author was given access to all of the royal gardens, and which included illustrations of him together with the King and Queen, could only have been produced in an era of popular monarchy. It is also indicative of

both George VI's personality and the dilemmas even the seemingly uncontroversial area of gardening produced for him as a popular monarch that he asked the author not to print the fact that he loathed rockeries (and indeed was dismantling the one at Royal Lodge) for fear of upsetting those who liked them.

On George VI's death his widow assumed the title of Queen Elizabeth, The Queen Mother and in the decades that followed she has never wavered in her gardening enthusiasm. Royal Lodge has been maintained as far as has been possible as it was during the King's lifetime, although economy has necessitated, for instance, replanting Russell Page's herbaceous garden with roses. Clarence House, her London residence, has only a small garden and is mainly notable for its two magnificent weeping plane trees which in summer act as canopies for outdoor receptions and luncheon parties. At Birkhall, on the Balmoral estate in Scotland, which she had used when Duchess of York, she has maintained and modified a garden laid out by Sir Dighton Probyn in the late Victorian style of the Scottish pleasaunce, a mixture of flowers, fruit and vegetables held together by a formal framework of hedges, paths and topiary. In 1952 she purchased the most northerly castle in Britain, Mey, where an old walled kitchen garden has been transformed into another pleasaunce subdivided by protective hedges, in which flowers, fruit and vegetables jostle in profusion.

To all of these gardens the Queen Mother has added her own distinctive touches, ones which are of planting rather than design. And the planting relates to her movements through the year to each of these residences: Clarence House and Royal Lodge from late autumn to early summer and the Castle of Mey and Birkhall in May from August to October, although there is usually a springtime visit to Birkhall too.

In her gardens the colour range is frequently pinks, blues and whites, both in scattered and in massed form. The style is of orchestrated profusion. The planting preferences are also consistent, making allowances for soil and climate. Always the emphasis is on anything scented, especially near the house where there is sure to be rosemary and lavender releasing their pungent aroma whenever brushed against. Magnolias, *Mahonia japonica,* philadelphus and the viburnums with their fragrant flowers abound, as do old roses, the centifolias, albas, damasks, Portlands and Bourbons, with their treasury of historic scent; whilst hyacinths, sweet peas, nasturtiums and scented geraniums feature among the flowers.

With George VI and Queen Elizabeth an enormous bridge has been crossed in the history of royal gardens. The gardens no longer seem set apart. They have ceased to be assertive or indeed intimidating and have become relaxed and welcoming. Their scale has dramatically diminished compared with the past. But the King and Queen had had to begin a painful period of adjustment and although brave decisions about the royal gardens had already been made by 1952, even braver ones would have to be made in the reign to come.

THE GARDEN OF THE CASTLE OF
Mey comes into its own
during August for the Queen
Mother's main annual visit.
Situated on an exposed
northerly coastline of Scotland,
the stone walls of the garden
ensure the microclimate and
provide protection from the
north-east wind, without
which any kind of flower
gardening would be almost
impossible. As some plants
flower here much later than
they do further south,
intriguing combinations occur
such as this one (*opposite*) of
nasturtiums with the pale pink
blooms of the climbing
'Albertine' rose. The paths of
this enclosure are covered in
white seashells.

AN AVENUE OF SYCAMORES (*right*)
forms a lacy arcade over the
drive at the Castle of Mey.

ECOLOGICAL NOSTALGIA

CHARLES, PRINCE OF WALES

With the death of George VI royal garden-making skips a generation to Charles, Prince of Wales (born 1948), and to his garden at Highgrove House, near Tetbury in Gloucestershire. This is a garden quite different from any of its royal predecessors and one being created in very different circumstances for the monarchy. It is the Queen who, since her accession as Elizabeth II in 1952 at the unexpectedly young age of twenty-five, has had to come to terms with a new era for the royal gardens. Brought up in the dutiful tradition exemplified by both her father and grandfather, and aided by an able and practical consort, Philip, Duke of Edinburgh, she has faced the painful necessity to cut back the royal gardens created by her predecessors. Although both lovers of country life and, in particular, of their two homes, Sandringham and Balmoral, to the Queen and the Duke of Edinburgh gardening has never been an overriding interest. She has nevertheless had to make more dramatic decisions about the royal gardens than any previous British monarchs. In a disheartening process, she has had to oversee the contraction of the area under cultivation and the grassing over of familiar

THE PRINCE OF WALES IN 1989; A DETAIL FROM A PORTRAIT BY TOM WOOD
which catches his pensive character questing a new role for the
monarchy as it moves into the twenty-first century.

THE POTAGER AT HIGHGROVE OWES ITS SATISFYING PROPORTIONS AND SENSE
of enclosure to the old eighteenth-century walled kitchen garden in
which it lies. Despite the almost overwhelming richness of the
planting, the design is held together by a firm sense of structure: the
focal point is a fountain protected by a white picket fence within a
circus of beds filled with herbs. These are contained by a circle of crab
apple trees whose branches are plaited to form, in spring, a crown of
flowers and, in autumn, one of golden fruits. One of the main dividing
paths leads to an inviting trellis arbour against the far wall.

BUCKINGHAM PALACE GARDEN IN the present reign, in spite of its role as a setting for the garden parties when the lawns have to withstand the onslaught of over 30,000 pairs of feet, as a helicopter landing pad and the intrusion of high rise blocks, still retains the quality of a private royal garden.

The forty verdant acres, a haven for wildflowers and life, provide space and air for the Queen to exercise her dogs, something which she does daily, following a more or less set route out through the entrance to the private apartments (*left above*) and along the winding walks laid out over a century and a half ago.

Both the Queen and her parents have added to the number of flowering trees and shrubs and as the gardens have become progressively overlooked, so other changes have been made in the planting to re-establish much-needed privacy. An avenue of Indian chestnuts, which form a green canopy in the summer, leads from a side door to the protection offered by the mature trees along the perimeter and a laburnum tunnel (*right*) provides a yellow-spangled arbour for the Queen in the late spring.

The Admiralty Pavilion (*far left below*), an eighteenth-century building attributed to William Kent, was placed here during the early years of this century; it makes a charming place from which to enjoy the view of the new rose garden.

The lake, originally excavated for George IV, has been enlivened by flamingoes since 1961 (*left below*).

flowerbeds, watching weeds run rampant and trees and shrubs go untended. Radical decisions have had to be made to reduce the labour force, adopt low-maintenance schemes such as groundcover planting, abandon uneconomical kitchen gardens in favour of buying in and demolish acres of greenhouses no longer tenable in terms of numbers of gardeners or, after the 1974 oil crisis, heating costs.

These developments have all taken place during the forty years of the present reign. The Victorian kitchen gardens at Frogmore and at Sandringham have had to be abandoned. Now all that can be seen at Frogmore of these once famous gardens are walled enclosures with handsome gate-piers surmounted by eagles with outspread wings looking down on the desolation. At Sandringham a few stray espaliered fruit trees still hug the brick walls and the now dry round basin and fountain remain to mark the crossing of the vanished herbaceous borders. The elaborate series of garden buildings are mostly given over to other uses but enough of their once greatly admired interior fittings remain to evoke the grape or fruit room as Edward VII would have known it. A sadder casualty is the Dairy and the Dutch Garden with its quaint turn-of-the-century topiary. The Square Garden and the pergola are now all that remain of the Victorian and Edwardian formal gardens. The forest of glass-houses in both places disappeared in the 1970s, giving place to fewer but more serviceable greenhouses in metal alloy, economically geared to produce flowers for the royal residences and state occasions and, in addition, for the commercial market. The accent has been on consolidation and streamlining, making use of any new labour-saving devices as they appear.

It is the Prince of Wales who has taken the innovatory role in royal gardening. Although he made his first garden as a child at Royal Lodge, if asked when he became interested in gardening, he would probably reply, in the same words as his grandfather, George VI: 'When I had a garden of my own.' That happened in 1981 when the Duchy of Cornwall purchased Highgrove, an estate of some four hundred acres. To put the Highgrove garden in historical perspective we need to look back to Sandringham and Royal Lodge, both creations of Princes who came to the throne. Sandringham had a hundred acres of pleasure grounds, Royal Lodge had fifteen or sixteen in its immediate vicinity, Highgrove has only about five. This dramatic reduction in scale is mirrored in the labour force: ninety at Sandringham in the 1890s, still over twenty at Royal Lodge as late as the early 1950s and today at Highgrove just two, plus a temporary trainee and one person full-time in the kitchen garden. In terms of royal garden history, both Highgrove's size and the number of gardeners are very modest. For a totally *new* garden in the 1980s, however, its scale can only be called brave.

Prince Charles inherits from his grandfather an interest in hands-on gardening and has thrown himself enthusiastically into every aspect of Highgrove's planning and planting. The garden is a personal expression of his visual taste and prefer-

ences and, at the same time, like every other royal garden in history, it is a child of its own time, capturing trends in garden style typical of the last two decades of the twentieth century. Highgrove is above all conceived as a classic country house garden, nostalgically looking back to the golden years before 1914 and the era of Gertrude Jekyll and Sir Edwin Lutyens. The revival of interest in their garden style and the cult of the country house reached their apogee during the 1980s with a spate of gardens that combined sound structure, both hard in the form of walls, paving, pavilions and statuary, and horticultural in the way of clipped hedges, avenues and topiary, with abundant planting in graduated colours to soften the lines.

Jekyll's profuse planting was based on cottage gardening, a style enthusiastically taken up in the 1970s and 1980s as part of the rural idyll. That in turn was linked with the steady rise of the ecological movement, to which the garden at Highgrove is a monument: no chemical sprays or artificial fertilizers are allowed. As a result the garden is a haven for the wildflowers, birds and insects decimated by intensive farming practices which have long since poisoned or destroyed the fields and hedgerows that were their natural habitat. It is a sanctuary too for some endangered plant species, in particular old varieties of apple. The decorative potager, a delightful mixture of flowers, fruit and vegetables, also became the height of garden fashion during the last decade, and Highgrove had an inspiring example in the much publicized one nearby at Barnsley House. And in its overall design too, Highgrove represents the recent swing of the pendulum towards formality, a movement which is still accelerating at the start of the 1990s. The Highgrove garden, to encapsulate it in one word, is eclectic.

Five people have advised or contributed in some way towards its making: Marjorie, known as Mollie, Marchioness of Salisbury, Vernon Russell-Smith, Miriam Rothschild (Mrs George Lane), Rosemary Verey and myself. What is striking about this group of people is that only one out of the five, Russell-Smith, is a garden designer by profession; all the rest are amateurs. The use of such a group not only draws on the personal abilities each has to offer but also, more importantly, preserves the Prince's prime role as the creator of his own domain, and it has been a combination of each person's predilections as a mirror of the Prince's own very definite tastes that has fashioned the garden.

In looking to amateurs the Prince of Wales is within the mainstream of what has happened to private garden design since 1900. Such people belong to a line of descent which goes back to Gertrude Jekyll, herself totally self-taught, and runs down through such major figures as Lawrence Johnston, Victoria Sackville-West and Margery Fish, all makers of seminal country house gardens: Munstead, Hidcote, Sissinghurst and Lambrook. Most of them were also writers, whose books remain influential.

The group involved at Highgrove represents different aspects

A SMALL, SIMPLE PRIVATE GARDEN for the royal family nestles beneath the protective walls of the East Terrace Garden at Windsor. An herbaceous border, a host of flowering climbers and some handsome specimen trees provide a succession of colour through the year, while a gothick aviary adds aural as well as visual interest.

PREVIOUS PAGES: THE ROSE GARDEN AT HIGHGROVE IS, IN SUMMER, PERHAPS
the epitome of the English ideal of a garden. Against a backdrop of
dark-green velvety yew is a cornucopia of old-fashioned roses and
plants; but what looks like artful profusion is tempered by a carefully
controlled palette of colour.

of today's garden style. Mollie Salisbury brought with her the garden experience from two great Jacobean houses, Cranborne Manor and Hatfield House, both residences of her husband's family, the Cecils, for four hundred years. This heritage has inevitably coloured her garden-making, which is a romantic reinterpretation of the style appropriate to the date of the buildings, that of the age of Shakespeare. The emphasis is heavily on pattern, with intricate knots and parterres, although the planting within is in the style we associate with the plantswoman, Gertrude Jekyll, that of soft graduated colour with plants in mingled if calculated profusion. Lady Salisbury was also a pioneer against all forms of chemical spray and fertilizers.

Rosemary Verey also belongs to the country house tradition but her work reveals the strong influence of the Arts and Crafts Movement with its stress on the use of natural materials. Her garden at Barnsley incorporates formal accents such as an avenue of stately Irish yews leading to a side door and a screen of pleached limes that flanks a laburnum tunnel, but is striking above all for its sophisticated planting and the way the asymmetrical delights of the cottage garden blend in with the manor house; while her simple potager, quartered and divided by narrow brick paths inspired by the early gardening writers, has become a standard reference. Miriam Rothschild embodies the ecological viewpoint. Hers has been a formidable voice ahead of its time and it is partly to her that we owe our present distrust of chemical sprays and our awareness of the need to preserve wildflowers and hedgerows and every living creature within them. As to my own stance, it is one perhaps which reminds gardeners that for centuries pleasure was derived not only from plants but from the year-round delights of structural elements: topiary, well-cut hedges, pleached trees, buildings and statuary.

Highgrove House, built between 1796 and 1798, is a handsome three-storey stone block in the classical style, to which classical pilasters and other architectural details have been added, providing character that was previously lacking. Nor in 1981 was there any garden to speak of. A wide gravel walk struck out from the rear façade of the house along its central axis, leading to a small rectangular pond on a raised mount. The path was flanked by golden yews, now of irregular shape but once neat clipped domes. On the greensward to either side there were handsome specimen trees, some of which dated back to the occupation of the house by Colonel Mitchell at the end of the last century. He was the founder of the famous arboretum at Westonbirt and these handsome mature trees immediately excited the Prince. Away from the house there was

a square walled enclosure which was the kitchen garden. But basically Highgrove was *tabula rasa* or, as the sale advertisement had put it, the house had 'easily maintained gardens'.

The initial planning of the garden was evolved between the Prince and Mollie Salisbury soon after the purchase and the great thrill of Highgrove is that it is a young garden, just over a decade old. It takes fifteen years for a garden to reach maturity and in an age of impatience and instant pleasures it is striking that such a time-span was accepted at the outset. The Prince's knowledge of plants and gardens has since developed hugely.

The garden he opted for looks above all to nearby Hidcote, Lawrence Johnston's Edwardian masterpiece, whose effects depend on the creation of garden 'rooms', each one calculated in terms of surprise and vista, as well as planting and seasonal variations of interest. So Highgrove began with the planting of yew hedges as walls, forming first one huge 'room' that encompasses not only existing specimen trees but also the back of the house, and secondly, at the side, a private rose garden. This creation of 'rooms' also conceals one of the disadvantages of the site: it is flat with no changes of level. At the same time the kitchen garden was laid out as a decorative potager for the raising of organic produce.

Every year at Highgrove there is the joy not only of seeing growth towards the completion of a composition but also of new projects. Even during the four years in which I have been involved, mainly in training the hedges and topiary, the changes have been great. Pretty gates designed by the Prince in what might be described as post-modernist gothick or Chinese Chippendale style have appeared. A serpentine tapestry hedge has suddenly wended its way across the grounds, giving subtle delineation where before there was none. Large handsome terracotta containers, trophies of royal travels, have appeared by seats or entrances, adding vertical accents. And I have sometimes encountered Rosemary Verey sitting pensively on a tree stump, considering how to place to advantage some new cornucopia of plants the Prince has acquired.

A garden tour that reveals Highgrove's eclecticism should start in the rose garden designed by Lady Salisbury, an essay in nostalgia, where a wide stone terrace on which to breakfast affords a glimpse through a rose-covered rustic arch along an avenue of crab-apple trees towards the kitchen garden. The rose garden is divided into quarters, with a sundial at its centre, and the beds are edged with lavender punctuated by domes of glossy green box. Within there is a tumbling mass of old roses and speciality varieties underplanted with a profusion of old-fashioned herbaceous plants. The accent is on softness of colour and on fragrance. That formula is repeated in a second small garden inspired by Lady Salisbury and planted by the Prince which forms a rustic terrace in mellow stone at the rear of the house. In the centre is a small fountain with entwined whales and to the sides are two tiny gothick pavilions which provide a place to shelter. Paving, walls and beds are filled with sprawling and rambling plants, above all scented ones: honeysuckle, roses, lavender, alchemilla, cottage pinks, with containers of daturas and pelargoniums added in summer.

Beyond that lies the great formal enclosure whose walls of rich dark-green yew are nearing completion; the walls have mighty buttresses and swags with arches and windows which give views on to the meadowland or provide gateways to other areas of the garden. Recently the Prince has transformed the dull central path into a more informal stone one flanked by many varieties of thyme, which in summer hum with the sound of bees and form a rich tapestry of greens, purples and yellows that marry with the inherited pre-1914 golden yews. On either side, the aerial clipped hedge of hornbeam supported by its avenue of trunks, inspired by neighbouring Hidcote, is slowly maturing, leading the eye past the boundaries of the enclosure along a lime avenue to a wooden dovecote. The hedge has four breaks in it where baroque stone statues of the Seasons from Italy are sited, adding an essential sculptural element, which is made more effective by the stone seats set into bays in the hedges. These too have been used as opportunities to create tableaux by planting flowering and fruit-bearing malus.

To one side of this formal enclosure is Rosemary Verey's cottage flower garden, which is both entered and left through rose-laden rustic arches in the manner of Humphry Repton. Here the mood changes from stately ordered symmetry to meandering informality: a grass path borders serpentine beds from which flowers cascade in profusion. It is a tiny garden crammed with herbaceous plants – hostas, euphorbia, lychnis, alchemilla mollis and a hundred others cheek by jowl. Beyond the furthest arch new planting schemes by Rosemary Verey and the Prince are under way to extend the flower garden. Crossing over the formal enclosure, through the gate opposite and on through the meadow dappled with wildflowers we reach the only uncontained garden at Highgrove, a woodland glade. Here the trees and shrubs are encircled by winding island beds filled with shade-loving plants – hostas, hellebores, foxgloves, tellima, cyclamen and hardy geraniums – with a boggy patch in the middle for water irises and gunnera.

Leaving the woodland glade we skirt the meadowland, with its groups of rare apple trees, and make our way along a sinuous path running beside a tapestry hedge, a mixture of deciduous and evergreen shrubs, yew, beech, holly, hornbeam and crataegus. The path gives delightful glimpses of the house and the formal gardens across the meadow, and halfway along there is a break where a comfortable seat, designed by the Prince, encircles the trunk of an ancient yew.

This path joins that from the Rose Garden leading towards the potager, which is approached by a gothick door inset into a gateway of warm ochre stone flanked by topiary sentinels. Beyond lies a gravel path flanked by huge terracotta containers that leads to a statue of Diana *à la chasse*. Halfway along, another gothick gate marks the entrance to the kitchen gardens.

The walls here already existed, so it is the most mature of all the gardens. Laid out to simple design by the Prince, the space is quartered and then quartered again diagonally. One main walk is an apple tunnel beneath which nasturtiums sprawl in late summer; the other is flanked by herbaceous borders. At the crossings in the quarters are large rose arbours and the paths leading to these may have arcades of sweet peas or runner beans, according to the season. Neatly clipped green box hedges hold in the beds and yew topiary figures, cut into the old-fashioned shapes seen in Cotswold gardens in the Victorian period, rise above the planting of flowers and vegetables.

Everything is lush, every wall supports roses, creating a waterfall of pink, cream and apricot bloom above beds whose herbaceous plants spill pell-mell across the paths. This must be the most beautiful kitchen garden of its period. And the whole garden must rank already – for it is still in the making – as a perfect microcosm of its era, paving the way from the twentieth into the twenty-first century.

One day Highgrove's owner will succeed as a monarch with a gardening commitment. In his hands the royal gardens which remain in the possession of the royal family will be safe. The others will enjoy whatever fate is meted out to them by government. Collectively, however, the royal gardens remain unique in their continuity over the past four centuries. What is so striking is how vividly they have reflected the personalities of their creators: the love of flowers of queens like Mary II, Charlotte or Alexandra, the intellectual quests of Caroline of Ansbach, the pretensions to regal dominance of Charles II and William III, the egotistical impulses of the decorator monarch, George IV, or the more domestic idylls of Victoria and Albert or George VI and the Queen Mother. Most of the great names in garden history are there: André Mollet, Daniel Marot, George London and Henry Wise, Charles Bridgeman, William Kent, 'Capability' Brown, Sir William Chambers, Sir Joseph Banks, Humphry Repton, John Nash and Sir Geoffrey Jellicoe. This is a mighty heritage and yet in many ways a forgotten one.

We live in a new age of garden history; conservation and restoration are the keynotes of this century. The royal gardens are as important as any of the royal palaces and need to be accorded the same degree of sensitive care and consideration. They are also the equal of any of the masterpieces in the Royal Collection. It seems ironic that the garden-loving British should have a long tradition of curators for the royal pictures and works of art but none for the gardens. Other royal gardens in Europe, those belonging to now vanished dynasties, are the subject of painstaking restoration to their pristine glory. If this book brings understanding and appreciation of our royal gardens, and stirs awareness of our need for constructive action to preserve and restore them, it will have achieved its objective.

BIBLIOGRAPHY

Virtually everything cited under each garden in Ray Desmond's *Bibliography of British Gardens*, St Paul's Bibliographies, London, 1984, has been consulted. In addition three other works proved of consistent use and are referred to in an abbreviated form below:

HENREY=Henrey, Blanche, *British Botanical Literature, before 1800*, Oxford, 1975

WORKS, V=Colvin, H.M., Crook, J. Mordaunt, Downes, Kerry and Newman, John, *The History of the King's Works*, ed. H.M. Colvin, London, 1976, V

WORKS, VI=Crook, J. Mordaunt, and Port, M.H., *The History of the King's Works*, ed. H.M. Colvin, London, 1973, VI

THE THEATRE OF THE COURT: CHARLES II

'The Anglo-Dutch Garden in the Age of William and Mary', *Journal of Garden History*, VIII, 1988, nos. 2–3, nos. 84, 97

BATEY, Mavis, and LAMBERT, David, *The English Garden Tour*, London, 1990 pp. 65–70

CROFT-MURRAY, Edward, *Decorative Painting in England 1537–1837*, I, London, 1962, pp. 50–60

The Diary of John Evelyn, ed. E.S. de Beer, Oxford, 1959

The Glory of the Garden, Exhibition, Sotheby's, London, 1987, no. 39

GREEN, David, *Gardener to Queen Anne*, Oxford, 1956, ch. VII–IX

GREEN, David, 'Planners of Royal Parks', *Country Life*, 1 March 1956, pp. 372–3

HAZELHURST, F. Hamilton, *Gardens of Illusion: The Genius of André Le Nostre*, New York, 1980, pp. 337–79

HENREY, I, pp. 175–77, 181–2, 200–3

JACQUES, David, and HORST, Arend van der, *The Gardens of William and Mary*, London, 1988, pp. 18–22, 30–1

KARLING, Sten, 'The Importance of André Mollet and His Family for the Development of the French Formal Garden', in *The French Formal Garden*, Dumbarton Oaks Colloquium on the History of Landscape Design, III, 1974, pp. 3–25

Land Use Consultants, 'Royal Parks Historical Survey: Hampton Court and Bushy Park', for the Department of the Environment, London, 1982

Land Use Consultants, 'Royal Parks Survey: Greenwich Park', for the Department of the Environment, London, 1985

LASDUN, Susan, *The English Park: Royal, Public and Private*, London, 1991, ch. 5

MILLAR, Oliver, *Tudor, Stuart and Early Georgian Pictures in the Royal Collection*, London, 1963, pp. 136–7 (316)

The Diary of Samuel Pepys, ed. Robert Latham and William Matthews, London, 1968–1978

SUMMERSON, John, *Architecture in Britain 1530–1830*, London, 1963 edn., pp. 109–11

WOODBRIDGE, Kenneth, *Princely Gardens: The Origins and Development of the French Formal Garden Style*, London, 1986, chs 7–11

WORKS, V, pp. 140–52, 153, 313–29

Wren Society, VIII, 1931

PRODIGALITY AND POWER: WILLIAM III, MARY II AND QUEEN ANNE

'The Anglo-Dutch Garden in the Age of William and Mary', *Journal of Garden History*, VIII, 1988, nos. 2–3

ARCHER, Michael, 'Pyramids and Pagodas for Flowers', *Country Life*, 22 January 1976, pp. 166–9

BATEY, Mavis, *The English Garden Tour*, London, 1990, pp. 84–9

FAULKENER, P.A., 'Notes on the Gardens of Kensington Palace', *Journal of the British Archaeological Association*, 3rd series, XIV, 1951, pp. 8–9

GREEN, David, *Gardener to Queen Anne*, Oxford, 1956

GREEN, David, *Queen Anne*, London, 1970, p. 100

HARRIS, John, *The Artist and the Country House: A History of Country House and Garden View Painting 1540–1870*, London, 1979, pp. 120 (117), 129 (130)

HARRIS, John, *William Talman: Maverick Architect*, London, 1982, pp. 43–5

HOPPER, Florence, 'Daniel Marot: A French Garden Designer in Holland', in *The Dutch Garden in the Seventeenth Century*, ed. John Dixon Hunt, Dumbarton Oaks Colloquium on the History of Landscape Architecture, XII, 1990, pp. 131–58

JACQUES, David, and HORST, Arend van der, *The Gardens of William and Mary*, London, 1988, chs 3 and 4

Land Use Consultants, 'Royal Parks Historical Survey: Hampton Court and Bushy Park', for the Department of the Environment, London, 1982

LAW, E., *History of Hampton Court Palace*, London, 1894, III

MILLAR, Oliver, *Tudor, Stuart and Early Georgian Pictures in the Royal Collection*, London, 1963, pp. 157–8 (423)

STANDBERG, Runar, 'The French Formal Garden after Le Nostre', in *The French Formal Garden*, Dumbarton Oaks Colloquium on the History of Landscape Design, III, 1974, pp. 41–67

WHINNEY, Margaret, 'William Talman', *Journal of the Warburg and Courtauld Institutes*, XVIII, 1955, pp. 123–39

ZEE, Henri and Barbara van der, *William and Mary*, London, 1973

GARDENS OF THE MIND: QUEEN CAROLINE

BEAN, W.J., *The Royal Botanic Gardens, Kew*, London, 1908, pp. 4–10

BLUNT, Wilfred, *In For a Penny*, London, 1978, pp. 1–13

COLTON, Judith, 'Kent's Hermitage for Queen Caroline at Richmond', *Architectura*, II, 1974, pp. 181–91

COLTON, Judith, 'Merlin's Cave and Queen Caroline: Garden Art as Political Propaganda', *Eighteenth Century Studies*, X, 1976, pp. 1–20

A Description of the Royal Gardens at Richmond in Surry . . ., not dated but probably *c.*1740 reprinted in *The English Landscape Garden*, ed. John Dixon Hunt, New York, 1982

EUSTACE, John, 'The Antinatural Style', in *The Rococo in England*, ed. Charles Read, London, 1984, pp. 8–20

HENREY, II, p. 501

HUNT, John Dixon, *William Kent: Landscape Garden Designer*, London, 1987, pp. 62–5

JACQUES, David, *Georgian Gardens: The Reign of Nature*, London, 1983, pp. 22, 31, 35

Land Use Consultants, 'Royal Parks Surrey: Kensington Gardens', for the Department of the Environment, London, 1982

MILLAR, Oliver, *Tudor, Stuart and Early Georgian Pictures in the Royal Collection*, London, 1963, I, p. 184 (559)

QUENNELL, Peter, *Caroline of England: An Augustan Portrait*, London, 1939

RORSCHACH, Kimerly, *The Early Georgian Landscape Garden*, Exhibition catalogue, Yale Center for British Art, New Haven, 1983, pp. 59–63

RUTTON, W.L. 'The Making of Kensington Gardens', *The Home Counties Magazine*, VI, 1904, pp. 145–59

A Tercentenary Tribute to William Kent, Exhibition catalogue, Ferens Art Gallery, Kingston upon Hull and University Gallery, Nottingham, 1985

WARD, Cyril, *Royal Gardens*, London, 1912, pp. 82–90

WEBB, M.I., *Michael Rysbrack: Sculptor*, London, 1954, pp. 145–54

WILKINS, W.H., *Caroline the Illustrious*, London, 1904

WILLIS, Peter, 'Charles Bridgeman: The Royal Gardens', in *Furor Hortensis: Essays on the History of the English Landscape in memory of H.F. Clark*, ed. Peter Willis, Edinburgh, 1974, pp. 41–7

WILLIS, Peter, *Charles Bridgeman and the English Landscape Garden*, London, 1977, pp. 90–7

WIMMER, C.A., and SCHAEFER, 'Charlottenburg's French Garden', *Journal of Garden History*, V, 1985, pp. 321–35

WORKS, VI, pp. 183–203, 217–24

THE IMPERIAL THEME: PRINCESS AUGUSTA

BEAN, W.J., *The Royal Botanic Gardens, Kew*, London, 1908, pp. 11–17

BLUNT, Wilfred, *In For a Penny*, London, 1978, pp. 14–44

BRYANT, Julius and COLSON, Carol, *The Landscape of Kenwood*, Exhibition catalogue, English Heritage, 1990

A Description of the Gardens and Buildings at Kew, in Surry . . . Brentford, not dated, but late 1760s reprinted in *The English Landscape Garden*, ed. John Dixon Hunt, New York, 1982

HARRIS, John, *The Artist and the Country House: A History of Country House and Garden View Painting in Britain, 1540–1870*, London, 1979, pp. 198–9, (203–4)

HARRIS, John, 'Exoticism at Kew', *Apollo*, LXXVIII, 1963, pp. 103–8

HARRIS, John, *Gardens of Delight: The Rococo English Landscape Gardens of Thomas Robins the Elder*, London, 1978, pp. 11–18

HARRIS, John, *Sir William Chambers: Knight of the Polar Star*, London, 1970, pp. 32–9, 212–4

HARRIS, John, 'Some Imperfect Ideas on the Genesis of the Loudonesque Flower Garden', in *John Claudius Loudon and the Early Nineteenth Century in Britain*, Dumbarton Oaks Colloquium on the History of Landscape Architecture, ed. Elisabeth B. MacDougall, 1980, pp. 47–57

HARRIS, John, 'William Kent and Carlton House Garden', *Apollo* CXXXIV, 1991, pp. 251–3

HARVEY, John, 'A Scottish Botanist in London in 1766', *Garden History*, IX, 1981, pp. 52–5

HENNEBO, Dieter, 'Tendencies in Mid-Eighteenth Century German Gardening', *Journal of Garden History*, V, 1985, pp. 350–70

HENREY, II, pp. 90–109, 241–5

HERVEY, Lord, *Lord Hervey's Memoirs*, ed. Romney Sedgwick, London, 1963 edn.

HONOUR, Hugh, *Chinoiserie: The Vision of Cathay*, London, 1961, pp. 143–74

JACQUES, David, *Georgian Gardens: The Reign of Nature*, London, 1983, pp. 73–8

JONES, Stephen, 'Frederick Prince of Wales: A Patron of the Rococo', in *The in Rococo in England: A Symposium*, ed. Charles Hind, London, 1986, pp. 106–12

MCCARTHAY, Michael, *The Origins of the Gothic Revival*, New Haven and London, 1987, pp. 17–23, 57, 105–15

MILLAR, Oliver, *The Queen's Pictures*, London, 1977, pp. 96–105

QUENNELL, Peter, *Caroline of England: An Augustan Portrait*, London, 1939

ROBERTS, Jane, *Royal Artists*, London, 1987, pp. 59–60

RORSCHACH, Kimerly, *The Early Georgian Landscape Garden*, Exhibition catalogue, Yale Center for British Art, New Haven, 1983, pp. 65–73

RORSCHACH, Kimerly, 'Frederick, Prince of Wales. Taste, Politics and Power', *Apollo*, CXXXIV, 1991, pp. 329–45

STROUD, Dorothy, *Capability Brown*, London, 1975 edn., pp. 133–4, 177–9

VERTUE, George, *Notebooks*, I, *Walpole Society*, XVIII, 1930, pp. 13–14

WIEBENSON, *The Picturesque Garden in France*, Princeton, 1978, pp. 23–38

WORKS, VI, pp. 138–9, 217–21

ROYAL BOTANIZING: QUEEN CHARLOTTE

BEAN, W.J., *The Royal Botanic Gardens, Kew*, London, 1908, pp. 18–24

BLUNT, Wilfred, *In For a Penny*, London, 1978, pp. 44 ff

CARTER, H.B., *Sir Joseph Banks 1743–1820*, London, 1988, pp. 96, 142, 171, 302–4, 409–10, 494–7

CORNFORTH, John, 'Frogmore House, Berkshire', *Country Life*, 16 August 1990, pp. 46–50

HAYDEN, Ruth, *Mrs Delaney, her Life and her Flowers*, Colonnade, 1980, pp. 131 ff

HEDLEY, Olwen, *Round and About Windsor*, 1948, s.v. Frogmore

HEDLEY, Olwen, *Queen Charlotte*, London, 1975, pp. 84–5, 113–14, 129–30, 137–8, 179, 185, 227, 233–4, 259, 306–7

HENREY, II, pp. 63, 75, 248, 253, 577

HINDE, Thomas, *Capability Brown: The Story of a Master Gardener*, London, 1986, pp. 100–5

Inventory of Frogmore, 23 February 1841 (kindly communicated by Jane Roberts)

JACQUES, David, *Georgian Gardens: The Reign of Nature*, London, 1983, pp. 82, 156

OPPÉ, A.P., *English Drawings: Stuart and Georgian Periods in the Collection of H.M. The King at Windsor Castle*, London, 1950, pp. 20 (7), 22 (18–20)

ROBERTS, Jane, *Royal Artists*, London, 1987, pp. 65–88

STROUD, Dorothy, *Capability Brown*, London, 1975 edn., pp. 123–4

WORKS, VI, pp. 133–8, 224–9

FASHION AND FORMALITY: GEORGE IV

AVERY, Charles, 'Hubert Le Sueur, the "Unworthy Praxiteles" of King Charles I', *Walpole Society*, XLVIII, 1980–82, pp. 35–209

BAILEY, Mavis, 'Regency Setting Restored', *Country Life*, 175, 1984, pp. 1152–4

BELLAIGUE, Geoffrey de, *Carlton House: The Past Glories of George IV's Palace*, Exhibition catalogue, Queen's Gallery, London, 1991

CARTER, George, GOODE, Patrick and LAURIE, Kedrun, *Humphry Repton: Landscape Designer*, Exhibition catalogue, Sainsbury Centre for Visual Arts, University of East Anglia, 1982–83

COATS, Peter, *The Gardens of Buckingham Palace*, London, 1978, ch. 9

Country Life, 1 July 1939, pp. 706–12

CHAMBERS, G.E., 'The "Ruins" at Virginia Water', *The Berkshire Archaeological Society*, LIV, 1954–5, pp. 39–52

CONNER, Patrick, 'The "Chinese Garden" in Regency England', *Garden History*, XIV, 1986, pp. 42–9

The Craces: Royal Decorators 1768–1899, ed. Megan Aldrich, Exhibition catalogue, The Royal Pavilion, Art Gallery and Museum, Brighton, 1990, pp. 27 ff

DENNIS, J., *The Landscape Gardener*, London, 1835, pp. 103–6

DINKEL, John, *The Royal Pavilion Brighton*, London, 1983

FARRANT, Sue, 'The Physical Development of the Royal Pavilion Estate and its influence on Brighton (E.Sussex)', *Sussex Archaeological Collections*, 120, 1982, pp. 171–84

Gardener's Magazine, 4, 1828, p. 177; 5, 1829, pp. 604–7; 14, 1837, p. 469

HARRIS, John, *A Catalogue of British Drawings for Architecture, Decoration, Sculpture and Landscape Gardening, 1550–1900, in American Collections*, New Jersey, 1971, s.v. Crace, Sandby

HARRIS, John, BELLAIGUE, Geoffrey de and MILLAR, Oliver, *Buckingham Palace*, London, 1968, part 1

HENREY, II, pp. 247, 253

HIBBERT, Christopher, *George IV, Prince of Wales*, London, 1972

HIBBERT, Christopher, *George IV*, London, 1973

HONOUR, Hugh, *Chinoiserie: The Vision of Cathay*, London, 1961, pp. 162, 186 ff

JACQUES, David, *Georgian Gardens: The Reign of Nature*, London, 1983, pp. 64–5, 112 f, 140, 185 f, 192, 202–3

JONES, Barbara, *Follies and Grottoes*, London, 1974 edn., pp. 141–2

LASDUN, Susan, *The English Park: Royal, Public and Private*, London, 1991, pp. 75, 126 ff

MACNAGHTEN, Angus, 'When Leptis Magna Came to Surrey', *Country Life*, 142, 1967, pp. 130–1

MALINS, Edward, 'Indian Influences on English Houses and Gardens at the beginning of the Nineteenth Century', *Garden History*, VIII, no. 1, 1980, pp. 44–66

MANSBRIDGE, John, *John Nash: A Complete Catalogue*, Oxford, 1991, pp. 175–6, 192, 197, 198–9, 274–6

MORLEY, John, *The Making of the Royal Pavilion Brighton*, London, 1984

MORSHEAD, Owen, *George IV and Royal Lodge*, Regency Society of Brighton and Hove, 1965

NASH, John, *Views of the Royal Pavilion*, Commentary by Gervase Jackson-Stops, London, 1991

OPPÉ, A.P., *English Drawings: Stuart and Georgian Periods in the Collection of H.M. The King at Windsor Castle*, London, 1950, p. 41 (179)

Proceedings of the Linnean Society of London, II, 1855, pp. 82–3

ROWAN, Alastair, *Garden Buildings*, RIBA Drawings Series, 1968, p. 60

SCOTT-ELLIOTT, A., "The Statues by Francavilla in the Royal Collection', *Burlington Magazine*, XCVIII, 1959, pp. 77–84

SMITH, H. Clifford, *Buckingham Palace*, London, 1931, pp. 65–6

STROUD, Dorothy, *Capability Brown*, London, 1975 edn., p. 232

STROUD, Dorothy, *Henry Holland*, London, 1950

STROUD, Dorothy, *Humphry Repton*, London, 1962, pp. 105, 131, 171

SUMMERSON, John, *John Nash*, London, 1980 edn.

WILLSON, E.J., *West London Nursery Gardens*, Fulham and Hammersmith Historical Society, 1982, p. 95

WOODS, May, and VARREN, Arete Swarz, *Glass Houses*, London, 1988, pp. 101–3

WORKS, VI, pp. 395–8

TASTE AND MEMORY: QUEEN VICTORIA AND PRINCE ALBERT

AMES, Winslow, *Prince Albert and Victorian Taste*, London, 1967

BRIGGS, Asa, 'Prince Albert and the Arts and Sciences', in *Prince Albert and the Victorian Age*, ed. John A.S. Phillips, Cambridge, 1981, pp. 51–78

BROWN, Ivor, *Balmoral: The History of a Home*, London, 1966

CAMPBELL, Susan, 'The Genesis of Queen Victoria's Great New Kitchen Garden', *Garden History*, XII, no. 2., 1984, pp. 101–19

CLARK, Ronald, W., *Balmoral: Queen Victoria's Highland Home*, London, 1981

DAVIS, John, *Antique Garden Ornament*, London, 1991, s.v. Austin & Seely, Coalbrookdale, Moritz Geiss

DUFF, David, *Victoria in the Highlands*, London, 1968

ELLIOTT, Brent, *Victorian Gardens*, London, 1986

FLORANCE, Arnold, *Queen Victoria at Osborne*, London, 1987

Gardeners' Chronicle, 1876, II, pp. 519–20; 19 June 1897, I, pp. 196–7

HARRIS, John, BELLAIGUE, Geoffrey de, and MILLAR, Oliver, *Buckingham Palace*, London, 1968, pp. 96–7

HOBHOUSE, Hermione, *Prince Albert: His Life and Work*, London, 1983, pp. 127–31, 139–45, 161–3

HOBHOUSE, Hermione, *Thomas Cubitt: Master Builder*, London, 1971, pp. 373 ff

Journal of Horticulture and Cottage Gardener, n.s., 34, 1897, pp. 563–6; 42, 1901, pp. 90–2

MACKWORTH-YOUNG, Robin, 'Queen Victoria and Prince Albert in Coburg", in *Prince Albert and the Victorian Age*, ed. John A.S. Phillips, Cambridge, 1981, pp. 79–110

MARTIN, Arthur Patchett, *The Queen in the Isle of Wight: A Personal Memoir of Her Majesty at Osborne*, London, 1898

MATSON, John, *Dear Osborne*, London, 1979

MILLAR, Delia, *Queen Victoria's Life in the Highlands as Depicted by her Watercolour Artists*, London, 1985

ROBSON, Eric, 'Where Wildness Remains Essential. Royal Gardens in Scotland', *Country Life*, CLXI, 1977, pp. 1382–6

A Summary of the Various Works Proposed and Executed on the Osborne Estate From 1845 to 1861 inclusive, By Direction of H.R.H. The Prince Consort . . ., 1880

WARD, Cyril, *Royal Gardens*, London, 1912, pp. 61–72

YORK, Duchess of and STONEY, Benita, *Victoria and Albert: Life at Osborne*, London, 1991

ABUNDANCE AND SILENCE: QUEEN ALEXANDRA

BATTISCOMBE, Georgina, *Queen Alexandra*, London, 1967

CATHCART, Helen, *Sandringham: The Story of a Royal House*, London, 1964

Country Life, 21 June 1902, pp. 806–18; 26 July 1902, pp. 105–6; 3 June 1923, pp. 301–06; 3 February 1934, pp. 116–39; 4 May 1935, pp. 452–54; 19 June 1980, pp. 319–21

DAVIS, John, *Antique Garden Ornament*, London, 1991, pp. 186 ff

ELLIOTT, Brent, *Victorian Gardens*, London, 1986, pp. 147, 166–7

FESTING, Sally, 'Great Credit upon the ingenuity and taste of Mr. Pulham', *Garden History*, XV, no. 1, 1988, pp. 90–102

The Gardeners' Chronicle, 20 June 1891, pp. 759–60; 3 September 1892, pp. 267–8; 21 June 1902, pp. 402–11; 16 August 1902, pp. 118, 355; 23 December 1905, p. 440; 17 February 1906, p. 104

Journal of Horticulture and Cottage Gardener, 18 January, 1872, pp. 59–62; 1 February 1872, p. 103–6

Journal of the Royal Horticultural Society, 1932, pp. 165–74

MAGNUS, Philip, *King Edward the Seventh*, London, 1964

MAWSON, Thomas, *The Life and Work of an English Landscape Architect*, London, 1927, pp. 157–8

MORGAN, John and RICHARDS, Alison, *A Paradise out of a Common Field*, London, 1990

OTTEWILL, David, *The Edwardian Garden*, London, 1989, pp. 13, 54, 204 n.67, 207 n.26

POPE-HENNESSY, James, *Queen Mary 1867–1953*, London, 1959

ROSE, Kenneth, *Kings, Queens and Courtiers*, London, 1986 edn., s.v. Alexandra, Probyn

WARD, Cyril, *Royal Gardens*, London, 1912, pp. 121–46

PRIVACY AND RETRENCHMENT: GEORGE VI AND QUEEN ELIZABETH

BRADFORD, Sarah, *George VI*, London, 1989, pp. 170–1

BROWN, Jane, *The English Garden in Our Time from Gertrude Jekyll to Geoffrey Jellicoe*, Antique Collectors' Club, 1986, pp. 102–5

HUSSEY, Christopher, and TAYLOR, G.C., 'Royal Lodge', *Country Life*, 1 July 1939, pp. 706–12

JELLICOE, Geoffrey, 'Ronald Tree and the Gardens of Ditchley Park: The Human Face of History', *Garden History*, X, no. I, 1982, pp. 80–91

PLUMPTRE, George, *Royal Gardens*, London, 1981, s.v. Royal Lodge, Sandringham

ROPER, Lanning, *Royal Gardens*, London, 1953

ROPER, Lanning, *The Gardens of the Royal Park at Windsor*, Reprint Society edn., London, 1952, ch. 1

SALISBURY, Marchioness of, *The Gardens of Queen Elizabeth The Queen Mother*, London, 1988

SHELLELL-COOPER, W.E., *The Royal Gardeners*, London, 1952

INDEX OF NAMES AND PLACES

ACKNOWLEDGMENTS

A project of this kind inevitably involves the courtesy of many. In the first case I am deeply indebted to Her Majesty The Queen for graciously sanctioning the television series, and in addition for her gracious permission to use material from the Royal Archives. I am also grateful to various members of the Royal Household who facilitated visits to gardens or assisted my researches, in particular Hugh Roberts, Jane Roberts, Sir Geoffrey de Bellaigue, Lady de Bellaigue, John Haslam and Felicity Murdo-Smith. Without the Lindley Library and Dr Brent Elliott this book would never have been written. Andrew Lawson has responded to my theme with painterly pictures and Prue Bucknall, the designer, has orchestrated the text and pictures with her usual flair. The real heroes of this book are, however, the gardeners themselves.

Roy Strong

The publishers would particularly like to thank Gwyneth Campling at the Royal Library and Frances Dimond at the Royal Archives for their unstinting help in providing photographs.

The publishers thank the following photographers and organizations for their kind permission to reproduce the photographs in this book (*denotes that images have been slightly cropped):

9 By Courtesy of the Board of Trustees of the Victoria and Albert Museum; 11 above* and 11 below Windsor Castle, Royal Library © 1992 Her Majesty The Queen; 12* Courtesy of Berkeley Castle, Gloucestershire; 14–15 Roger Last; 15 right The Royal Collection, St James's Palace © Her Majesty The Queen; 18 above The National Maritime Museum, Greenwich; 18 below Bibliotheque de L'Institut de France, Paris (Jean-Loup Charmet); 19 Aerofilms Ltd.; 21 The Royal Collection, St. James's Palace © Her Majesty The Queen; 22 Algemeen Rijksarchief, The Hague; 25 below right Stichting Atlas van Stolk, Rotterdam; 26–7* The Royal Collection, St. James's Palace © Her Majesty The Queen; 28 Aerofilms Ltd.; 30* Courtesy of the Masters and Fellows of Magdalene College; 35 above Kensington Public Library; 37 The Royal Collection, St James's Palace © Her Majesty The Queen; 41 above* Kensington Public Library; 41 below Aerofilms Ltd.; 42 Kensington Public Library; 43 below Reproduced by Courtesy of the Trustees of the British Museum; 46–7 The Royal Botanic Gardens, Kew; 47 right The British Library; 49 The Royal Collection, St. James's Palace © Her Majesty The Queen; 51 above* Reproduced by Courtesy of the Trustees of the British Museum; 52–3* Windsor Castle, Royal Library © 1992 Her Majesty The Queen; 53 right* The Royal Botanic Gardens, Kew; 54 Robert O'Dea; 60 above* Private Collection/Bridgeman Art Library; 62–3 The Metropolitan Museum of Art, Harris Brisbane Dick Fund, 1925; 65 The Royal Collection, St James's Palace © Her Majesty The Queen; 68 above Reproduced by Courtesy of the Trustees of the British Museum; 68 below* Windsor Castle, Royal Library © 1992 Her Majesty The Queen; 69 above* and 69 below Windsor Castle, Royal Library © 1992 Her Majesty the Queen; 70* Windsor Castle, Royal Library © 1992 Her Majesty The Queen 73 below *Country Life*; 74–5 Windsor Castle, Royal Library © 1992 Her Majesty The Queen; 79 The National Portrait Gallery, London; 80–3* Windsor Castle, Royal Library © 1992 Her Majesty The Queen; 85 below* Brighton Borough Council; 86 Reproduced by Courtesy of the Trustees of the British Museum; 87–8* Windsor Castle, Royal Library © 1992 Her Majesty The Queen; 91 below Windsor Castle, Royal Library © 1992 Her Majesty The Queen; 93 below* Windsor Castle, Royal Library © 1992 Her Majesty The Queen; 94 below left Aerofilms Ltd.; 94 below right Courtesy of the Lindley Library, Royal Horticultural Society; 95 right *Country Life*; 96 Windsor Castle, Royal Library © 1992 Her Majesty The Queen; 97 above Aerofilms Ltd.; 97 below Courtesy of the Lindley Library, Royal Horticultural Society; 103 The Royal Collection, St. James's Palace © Her Majesty The Queen; 104–5 Courtesy of Mr A. Wilkie; 106 Windsor Castle, Royal Library © 1992 Her Majesty The Queen; 107 Windsor Castle, Royal Archives, © 1992 Her Majesty The Queen; 108 left* Windsor Castle, Royal Library © 1992 Her Majesty The Queen; 109 below* Windsor Castle, Royal Library © 1992 Her Majesty The Queen; 110 below* Windsor Castle, Royal Library © 1992 Her Majesty The Queen; 111 below Windsor Castle, Royal Library © 1992 Her Majesty The Queen; 112 below From *Antique Garden Ornament* by John Davis (Reproduced by permission of The Antiques Collectors' Club, Suffolk); 114 above The Royal Collection, St James's Palace © Her Majesty The Queen; 114 below* Windsor Castle, Royal Archives © 1992 Her Majesty The Queen; 115 Windsor Castle, Royal Library © 1992 Her Majesty The Queen; 122* Windsor Castle, Royal Archives © 1992 Her Majesty The Queen; 124 below Windsor Castle, Royal Library © 1992 Her Majesty The Queen; 127 The Royal Collection, St. James's Palace © Her Majesty The Queen; 128* Windsor Castle, Royal Archives © 1992 Her Majesty The Queen; 129 The Hulton Deutsch Collection; 131 From *Royal Gardens* by Cyril Ward 1912 Longmans; 134* Windsor Castle, Royal Archives © 1992 Her Majesty The Queen; 135 below* Windsor Castle, Royal Archives © Her Majesty The Queen; 136* Windsor Castle, Royal Library © 1992 Her Majesty The Queen; 137 above *Country Life*; 137 below* Windsor Castle, Royal Archives © 1992 Her Majesty The Queen; 139 The Royal Collection, St James's Palace © Her Majesty The Queen; 140–1 Roger Last © 1992 Her Majesty The Queen; 142 The Hulton Deutsch Collection; 143 above Roger Last © 1992 Her Majesty The Queen; 144 Aerofilms Ltd.; 150–1 Derry Moore; 153 Courtesy of Sheeran Lock Fine Art Consultants (Photograph courtesy of Tom Wood.).

The following photographs were specially taken for Conran Octopus and BBC Books by Andrew Lawson:

1, 5, 20, 23, 25 above and below left, 29, 31, 32, 33, 35 below, 36, 43 above, 45, 48, 51 below, 56–9, 60 below, 66–7, 71, 78, 85 above, 108–9, 110 above, 111 above, 112 above, 113.

© 1992 Lord Chamberlain, 3, 6, 8, 13, 16, 17, 64, 73 above, 77, 89–90, 91 above, 92–3, 94 above, 95 above and below left, 98–9, 100–1, 102, 117–19, 120–1, 123, 124 above, 125–6, 130, 132–3, 135 above, 138, 140 left, 143 below, 145–7, 148–9, 154–9.

© 1992 A.G. Carrick Limited 2, 152, 158–9.